THE
SOLO
THOUGHT LEADER
FROM SOLOPRENEUR TO GO-TO EXPERT IN 7 STEPS

DIEGO PINEDA

VISION&LEADERSHIP
BOOKS

First Edition

Editing by Kelly Lydick
Cover designed using resources from Freepik.com

ISBN: 978-0-9937876-2-1

Vision & Leadership Books
Kelowna, BC, Canada

For Diana — my best student, the love of my life.

Contents

IS THIS BOOK
FOR YOU?

Chapter 0

What? Another book about thought leadership?

Hum, yeah. Well, add it to the pile.

Here's the thing though: I've read the other ones and they have some good stuff, but… it feels like they were written for lofty C-executives who hang out with angel investors and attend luxurious charity galas.

The truth is that, as a solopreneur, I could not relate to any of them. So, I decided to write the book I wanted to read. A book for the brave little guy and gal running their own businesses; those without big budgets or friends in high places. A book for the rest of us.

This is it. Hope you like it.

If you do, let's connect on LinkedIn, just send me a note. You can find me here: linkedin.com/in/dipineda/. And if you don't find the book useful, we can connect as well. I promise I won't hold it against you.

Cheers!

Diego Pineda

SOLO, BUT NOT ALONE

What is Solo Thought Leadership?

Chapter 1

How would it feel to be called the father or mother of a new industry?

Or even a sub-niche in your industry?

Amazing, wouldn't it?

We've all heard about Ogilvy, the father of advertising, or Edward Bernays, the father of Public Relations.

They were legends. Geniuses. How can we compare? Is it even possible?

I think it is.

Look at Seth Godin. He is known as the father of permission marketing, a close cousin to inbound marketing.

In the 1980s, Godin was in the advertising industry, where companies were blindly spending money on TV and print ads with no idea if their messages were effective or not.

In his own words, he was a witness to "a huge bonfire of money spent with no return on traditional advertising." [1]

Godin became a student of how companies used advertising and tested his own ideas to make it better.

In 1990, Prodigy hired his company to build a promotion for their online service. Instead of old fashion ads, they created Guts, "one of the very first online promotions." Basically, an email newsletter with coupons for subscribers.

The promotions worked so well that he was hired to do the same for AOL, Delphi, Apple, Microsoft, and CompuServe.

"I realized that my journey was a metaphor for what millions of marketers at millions of companies were doing, or were about to do," he said of that time. "I'd gone from spen-ding oodles of money in traditional advertising to building something completely different, vastly more efficient, and measurably more effective. We'd honed the idea of Permission Marketing." [2]

What is common sense to marketers today, that it's better to attract the attention of prospects through education instead of interrupting them with advertising, was his breakthrough idea.

He would later publish his book *Permission Marketing* and his company was later acquired by Yahoo! for $30 million.

Not bad, eh?

But that was just the beginning. Godin went on to write many more books, have the most read blog in the world, and be inducted in the Marketing Hall of Fame.

Seth Godin is a business thought leader because he chose the right path to thought leadership.

This is how he started:

• He studied his field until he was an advertising expert, realizing what worked and what didn't.
• He practiced and tested advertising and marketing ideas until he found new ways of doing things.
• He invented a new marketing category, built a business around it, and showed results.

So far so good: a successful business owner, but not a thought leader yet. But then he took the next steps:

He began educating and inspiring others through his books, his blog, videos, online courses and talks, creating raving fans around the world. And as a result, his business and income have grown exponentially.

- He has published 19 best-selling books, translated into 35 languages.
- More than 60,000 people have taken his online courses.
- He's in the Guerrilla Marketing Hall of Fame, the Direct Marketing Hall of Fame, and the Marketing Hall of Fame.
- A daily blog for over a decade with 7,500+ posts and more than a million readers.
- He can sell high-ticket items, like the altMBA, an online workshop that sells for $4,450 (5,000 people have graduated from the altMBA by the end of 2021). [3]

So, what is a thought leader? And what is a solo thought leader?

A thought leader is an expert who educates his or her audience to improve their businesses or their industry, and makes a lasting impact.

Some people mistakenly use the word "influencer" to refer to them, but being an influencer is not the same as being a thought leader. The Kardashians are influencers, but they're not thought leaders.

You don't follow them for their life-changing ideas.

B2C brands use influencers to get people to buy their products, but thought leaders use their influence to add value and produce lasting change.

In the B2B world, thought leader is a title reserved for someone with the power to persuade others and the status and authority to change the direction of a company or even an industry. Some examples include Gary Hamel, an American management consultant and the late Minoru Makihara, who was the chairman and CEO of the Mitsubishi Corporation.

In the academic world, a thought leader is usually a professor at a prestigious business school who does research and writes about a particular topic, such as the late Clay Christensen on innovation, or Michael Porter on strategy.

Until now, thought leaders have been those with important credentials and impressive resumes, like C-executives, famous consultants, or Ph.D.s from Harvard or Wharton.

But there is a new breed of thought leaders who are using digital media and virtual networks to spread new ideas and transform their fields. I call them Solo Thought Leaders.

Solo thought leadership is about:

Results, not degrees.
Passion, not trajectory.
Innovation, not formulas.
Experience, not credentials.
Educating others, not hoarding knowledge.
And overall, it is about execution.

It all starts in your own industry, learning the ropes, mastering the foundations. Then you can branch out into innovative ideas.

The Pathway to Innovation

Aspiring solo thought leaders can learn the pathway to innovation from jazz legend Clark Terry, who summed up the art of improvising in jazz into three steps: imitation, assimilation, and innovation.

1. Imitation

Just like jazz students choose a model to follow and imitate while learning the craft, you can start by imitating a successful innovator in your industry.

Ask yourself: Do I know all the details there are to know about my industry? Who are the innovators and experts from whom I can learn?

2. Assimilation

Musicians practice what they learn until it's ingrained to the point that they'll never forget it. Assimilate the basics of your industry and apply them in your business until you see results.

Ask yourself: Have I put into practice what I have learned about my business? Have I documented the results?

3. Innovation

Innovation in music happens after hours upon hours of imitation and assimilation. The same happens in business (although instead of hours, it takes years).

Leaning on your own practice and experiences, start branching out and trying new approaches to old problems.

Ask yourself: What is my stance on the different issues in my industry? Do I have a strong opinion about one of them?

"There's no disgrace for any kid today to copy what their idols did," said Clark Terry a few years ago. "Then after a certain point you can say, hey, I wonder what happens if I make a right turn here, let's see what happens if I make a left turn here. Then you are getting into innovation." [4]

As we saw with Seth Godin's story, and as I will insist in the rest of this book, it is not enough to become an expert or innovator if you don't educate others about it. Otherwise, you're a practitioner, not a thought leader.

If you have strong opinions and provocative ideas, the next questions you must ask yourself are: Are my opinions worth listening to? Can I communicate my ideas persuasively, both speaking and writing?

With the answers to these key questions you can create a following, a community around your ideas. You'll still be a solopreneur, but you won't be alone.

Why should I become a solo thought leader?

In his book *Good to Great*, Jim Collins, talks about the concept of the Hedgehog in relation to businesses. [5]

The origin of the concept is the Greek parable of the hedgehog and the fox, which shows that the winner is not always the biggest and strongest, but the one with a winning formula.

The story is about how the smart and agile fox decides to eat the hedgehog. Day after day the fox uses his superior skills to sneak up on the hedgehog with the same result: just when it looks like the fox is going to get him, the hedgehog rolls up into a little ball with his needles pointing straight out.

It doesn't matter how much better the fox is at everything else, it can't beat the hedgehog in this contest.

It is with the hedgehog strategy that the small, less resourced company or individual can outperform the bigger competitor.

Jim Collins defines the Hedgehog concept with three essential ingredients:

1. Passion

A Hedgehog must come from your passion, from something you want to give your energy to.

Business consultant, David Shriner-Cahn, says you need to understand what you most love to do and what you're most competent at doing. "If they're not the same," he says, "you need to find the intersection between the two, like in a Venn diagram, find the sweet spot." [6]

Not sure what you are passionate about because you have too many interests? Perhaps you are a multipotentialite, someone who has many interests, who knows about different things, even unrelated things.

And that's okay. It won't stop you from becoming a solo thought leader. Here's an exercise you can do, recommended by Steven Kotler in *The Art of Impossible*. [7]

Write down twenty-five things you are curious about, things you would read books or attend lectures about. Be as specific as possible. For example, instead of just listing NFTs, write down something like uses of NFTs for books (that's one of my interests, by the way).

Once you finish the list, look for places where these ideas intersect. Let's say you are also curious about the history of successful tech companies. Perhaps you can end up creating a startup in the NFT space dedicated to book publishing.

Kotler says that the intersection of different curiosity streams creates the conditions for the brain to recognize patterns and link ideas, which results in more dopamine in the brain. And the pleasurable feeling caused by dopamine is a key to passion. [8]

2. Economic Engine

A Hedgehog must drive the Economic Engine. In other words, it must be able to produce significant profit consistently.

In your search for a sub-niche with little or no competition, be careful not to end up where there are zero competitors, but also zero customers. In fact, a better way to drive your economic engine would be to narrow your niche to target customers who are willing to pay a premium price for a differentiated product or service that is not served in the current market.

3. Best in the world

A Hedgehog must position you as the best in the world at what you do. This does not mean the "whole world." It means being the best "in your world" as you define it.

Here's a good example from marketing thought leader, David Meerman Scott.

"There's probably more than 20,000 people in the United States who call themselves social media marketing experts," David says. "So, if you want to become a social media marketing expert, that's great, go for it. But does the world really need one more social media marketing expert?" [9]

According to David, it would be better for you to think, what am I really good at? What is my unique ability to make sense of the world? And can I create a business around something that only I can see and other people don't?

For example, could you be the world's number one expert on how dentists can use TikTok? That would be an interesting hedgehog, to say the least.

"In my case," says David, "I saw very early that marketing on the internet was not about advertising but about content creation. And that's what I wrote about for years, probably a thousand blog posts about that topic. It took a long time for people to consider that this idea made sense, but that's my own. I don't own it as in have a copyright over it, but I'm now known as someone who has been pioneering in that area and that allows me to be able to have a really interesting career as a result. If I had been doing what everybody else was doing, which was becoming an expert on banner ads, that never would have happened."

Defining a hedgehog is a lot like becoming a thought leader: it will establish you as an expert in an industry you are passionate about, which will create profits for you.

To summarize, becoming a thought leader for your niche will:

- Establish you as the expert—people in your niche will pick you over your competition every time.
- Simplify your marketing efforts—you only have to market to your niche and not mass market and get drowned in the noise.
- Allow you to charge higher prices—because you are the expert, you can charge premium fees for your product or service.

One great example of the latter is Peter Diamandis, a thought leader in the fields of innovation and disruptive technologies. After giving TED Talks, publishing three best-selling books, and spearheading high profile projects like the X Prize, Diamandis has established himself as an authority for tech entrepreneurs.

And one of the results? Annual membership to his mastermind, Abundance360, starts at $15,000 for virtual membership, with two upgrades for in-person attendance at $20,000 and $35,000 per year.

Not bad.

How do I become a solo thought leader?

Whether you're a business consultant, a career coach, or a solopreneur trying to make it online, you can also become a thought leader, following the 7 steps in this book.

1. **Become the go-to expert in your niche:** research and keep learning so you can charge higher prices for your services.

2. **Develop an angle for your message:** innovate and lead with a unique point of view, rising above the competition.

3. **Find your voice:** let your personality shine, stand out and remain top-of-mind.

4. **Educate your audience and dominate social media:** create and share valuable content, consistently; pick your social network(s) and build a strong presence and connections so people will listen to what you have to say.

5. **Gain visibility:** give massive value and let others sing your praises through social proof and media attention, building a community of loyal fans that will buy everything you release.

6. **Create scalable systems and processes:** set up a business that runs by itself so you'll have time to do the things that you love.

7. Write a book: gain instant authority and credibility with a published book.

This book is not like most business books out there (at least that's my intention and you'll judge if it is or not at the end).

For one, it's short. I hate fluff and will make my points without going in circles and repeating myself to meet a word quota. Second, unlike current books in the market, I won't try to impress you by citing hundreds of research articles to prove my points. No, this is a practical book so instead of consulting academic papers, I interviewed practitioners of thought leadership.

You'll read the stories and lessons of thought leaders who have gone through that path before you, including:

- Viveka von Rosen, who went from independent consultant to one of the top LinkedIn experts and then became Co-founder and Chief Visibility Officer of Vengreso, a digital sales training company.
- Justin Welsh, a former SaaS executive who left the corporate world to become a successful online solopreneur with a loyal community of followers.
- David Meerman Scott, a marketing guru and best-selling author of 16 books, whose innovative ideas make him a model for any aspiring thought leader.
- Jaime Jay, a former U.S. Army paratrooper who went from homeless to seven-figure entrepreneur.
- Bob Goodwin, a sales leader with a background in corporate America, who went solo to help others find their dream jobs.

- Megan Bowen, co-founder of Refine Labs, a B2B marketing agency that is revolutionizing the way companies do marketing.
- And others like John Arms, Marcus Chan, David Shriner-Cahn, and Bernie Borges, whose stories illuminate the exciting journey toward thought leadership.

So, are you ready to go from solopreneur to thought leader? It's a process of thinking, innovating, educating others, and leading. But overall it is about taking control of your destiny and creating your own future.

Let's go!

Checklist

☑ I have defined my hedgehog (niche).

☑ I am passionate about my niche.

☑ I have the potential of making a lot of money in my niche.

☑ I am or can become an expert (the best in my world) in my niche.

☑ I understand my business and industry deeply,

☑ I know the basics and the trends of my business,

☑ I know who the big players and thought leaders (innovators) are in my industry,

☑ I am a practitioner with results and not just an observer.

☑ I am documenting my journey and my results.

☑ I have a clear stance or strong opinion about important issues in my industry.

CONTENT MARKETING IS DYING. LONG LIVE THOUGHT LEADERSHIP.

Why you should bet on this

Chapter 2

When you hear about the "new big thing" on LinkedIn or Twitter, it's already too late. Those social media posts are telling you to do what everyone is already doing:

- Launch an online course.
- Create a personal brand.
- Record tons of videos.
- Build an email list.
- Start a podcast.
- Write a blog.
- Implement SEO.

Yeah, that's cool. Nothing wrong with that. So what?

- What nobody is saying:
- Find a mentor to learn from.
- Attend events outside your industry.
- Study trends and foresee a different future.
- Read authors with an opposite point of view to yours.
- Build or join a group of experts to bounce off new ideas.
- Test those new ideas by communicating them through different channels.

If you do the former you'll just be a thought follower; but if you do the latter, you'll become a Thought Leader.

Innovative ideas are not discussed on social media but on mastermind groups, private conversations between entrepreneurs, and brainstorming sessions among peers.

For instance, a few years ago, author James Altucher interviewed Peter Thiel, co-founder of PayPal and investor in companies like Facebook, SpaceX, and Palantir. James asked Thiel how he came up with ideas on a daily basis. And this is what he replied:

"You know, I spent today looking at a variety of financial technology opportunities. This morning we were sort of brainstorming in that space. There's probably a lot of opportunity there for reinventing what banks are, what finance does. I met a guy who's a founder of another finance tech company called Awonga in the UK. It's a sort of payday loans business. Then there's sort of a question, what one could do from there. And we just compared notes on what we thought was happening in the financial technology space. It was an extremely fruitful conversation." [1]

The fact is that if you want to break through the noise, you have to do something different than just scrolling through your Facebook feed.

Of course, following popular trends is easier, because you can see people are selling courses and making tons of money online (or so it seems), and if it worked for them, then it must work for you.

Since the mid 2000s, online marketers have been using "lead magnets" to entice people to give them their emails and contact info, so they can enter them into a funnel. It used to work wonders. In 2006, I began building an email list offering a free chapter of my $29 ebook and sold thousands of dollars to that list.

But today, people are usually annoyed when you ask them for their email to access their content and 75% won't even bother. Of the 25% who fill out the form, a good percentage will provide a fake email address or unsubscribe right after downloading the publication.

Let's be honest here. When was the last time you bought something or signed up for a service after reading a blog post or downloading an ebook?

Right. Never.

You probably were already seeking a solution to your problem, looked at a few websites, read reviews, asked your friends and family for recommendations, and then made an emotional decision based on a hunch.

And chances are, you bought from a known brand or someone you followed on social media and was top of mind. In other words, you bought from someone who had built some type of influence or thought leadership.

You may feel that building thought leadership and connecting with smart people to discuss business strategies on a daily basis is "too hard."

And you're right, it's not a walk in the park. But do you know what's harder?

- Trying to trick the ever-changing LinkedIn or Facebook algorithms.
- Tweaking and updating blog posts non-stop to climb Google ranks.
- Cold emailing contacts until you drop.
- Self-promoting the heck out of your coaching services.
- Obsessing over vanity metrics with no real revenue.

If you want to make an impact, you must stop doing the same things and expecting different results. Quit the content marketing rat race and become a solo thought leader in your own right.

Why Creating Content Isn't Enough

Content marketing (and marketing in general) is broken. The old ways don't work anymore.

Take for example, Search Engine Optimization (SEO), which is what you do to be found on search engines such as Google or Bing. A decade ago, you could add a few keywords to your blog posts, some backlinks, and voilà, you were on page one of Google's search results for your desired keywords.

In fact, when I started creating online content in 2004 for a non-profit, we didn't even think about keywords. We just wrote blog posts that we thought our readers would like and it worked—50,000 visitors per month through organic (not paid advertising) traffic.

Today, the market is so saturated that ranking for competitive words is extremely difficult for most and almost impossible for new websites with no domain authority.

"SEO is becoming harder and harder. It takes longer to rank and you have to spend more money to get results." That's a quote from Neil Patel, the guru of SEO. [2]

And it's even harder for small businesses and solopreneurs. On the one hand, they don't have the resources to hire an SEO agency or a full-time SEO specialist to keep up with the constant changes in the algorithms.

And on the other hand, because Google, just like people in general, favors known brands and publications over small businesses and little websites. Bigger brands have had more time to build an online presence, get quoted (and linked) in the media, buy expensive AI tools to optimize their content perfectly, and may even have a dedicated Google rep to help them out when rankings fall.

Let's say, for example, that you are a career coach and you wanted to be found in Google. With a monthly search volume of 22,000, it is very hard to rank for it; you would have to pay around $12 to get a click on an ad for it, and you'd need thousands of backlinks and a high domain authority to compete with the top sites ranking for that word.

Keyword overview for "career coach" at ubersuggest.com

As an independent coach, SEO is the least cost-effective strategy for getting new clients. And even for small companies, it won't be enough either.

A Tale of Two Companies

Not long ago, Nick (not his real name) was the Marketing Director at a B2B company. He had a well-thought out content marketing strategy based on Neil Patel's recommendations and implemented all the strategies and tactics for months, increasing traffic from 6,000 to 13,000 organic visitors per month. His team managed to rank 50 keywords on page one of Google.

They had more website visitors, more views of their content. But there was no impact on revenue. Why? Because competing for generic keywords brought unqualified leads, people looking for information, not people with buying intent.

"Let's focus on conversions," Nick told the team. "Let's improve the user experience on the website and add more focused calls to actions."

Still nothing.

But the CEO of the company insisted that the devil was in the details and they just needed to keep tweaking the blog. The CEO would email the marketing team in the middle of the night with instructions to update and refine stuff:

Make the site faster to load!
Add thirty to fifty internal links to every article!
Name every image the right way!
Embed more videos into the blog posts!
Change the headlines to match relevant search keywords!

"We were playing the SEO game," Nick says. "One day we were on page one of Google, the next one we dropped 20 spots. Rankings changed and we ended up spending hours adding keywords, headlines and links just to move up a notch temporarily. It was exhausting. The CEO was happy when we were up and perplexed when we went down. And he threatened to fire us if we missed a tiny SEO detail next time." [3]

The CEO could have used all that time he used obsessing over SEO, to come up with original thought leadership ideas and build the company's brand, creating a cult following.

"The funny thing was," Nick says, "that we got more traction from one of the CEO's LinkedIn posts than from our blog posts. He had a large following and influence, but he would only post every now and then. Despite all the work we put in every day, the company struggled to hit its revenue targets and marketing was always underperforming. At the end of the day, that focus on the details that didn't matter ended up burning out the marketing team and many got fired. I quit before it happened to me."

Contrast that story with another company, Refine Labs, and its CEO, Chris Walker.

Refine Labs does not publish a blog, nor do they do email marketing, or any SEO at all.

I asked Megan Bowen, COO & CCO at Refine Labs (and Chris Walker's founding partner) about the origin of their content strategy. She says that in 2019, Chris saw an opportunity with video on LinkedIn. He had been writing original content, but people were plagiarizing his text posts. In the meantime, not too many people were leveraging video.

So, he started recording videos by himself and posting them. His unique point of view started attracting followers. By early 2020, they decided to add a live event strategy with other LinkedIn influencers in different cities.

"The plan was to continue to execute that live event strategy," Megan says, "but then the pandemic happened and we moved to virtual events. So, the creation of the weekly demand gen live series is what then inspired the formal creation of the State of Demand Gen podcast in April 2020. And then it just became a natural flywheel, because you would record a long audio podcast episode, chop that up into five micro videos for LinkedIn and then just continue to do that over and over again." [4]

Chris records a 90-minute video podcast every week, where he interviews subject matter experts, or he provides the content himself, and then they distribute that piece of content through different channels:

- The audio file through podcast aggregators.
- Short video clips (3 to 7 minutes) on LinkedIn.
- Both long and short videos on YouTube and TikTok.

That's all they do and it works marvels for them. Chris is a marketing thought leader with a unique angle (more about that later) that has created a cult following on LinkedIn. He may not have as many followers as some influencers out there, but his audience is engaged and, most importantly, many companies have hired Refine Labs because of the podcast or the LinkedIn posts.

"The growth of the company has been incredible," Megan says. "We're 100% bootstrapped. A year-and-a-half ago we had about seven customers. Now, we have more than forty. Our prices have changed from ten thousand dollars a month to forty thousand dollars a month. We now have more than sixty people at the company and so the growth has been significant and we've been able to maintain and operate a profitable business from the beginning."

Solo Thought Leaders vs. Content Creators

There are five secrets every solo thought leader knows that regular content creators don't know:

One
Solo thought leaders dive deep into their niches to become the go-to experts.
Content creators create broad pillar topics to compete for search results.

Two
Solo thought leaders take a stand on their topics and aren't afraid of controversy.
Content creators present the pros and cons of a topic to let the reader decide.

Three
Solo thought leaders are passionate about building a community of engaged fans.
Content creators are obsessed with likes and post views.

Four

Solo thought leaders develop a unique voice and style for their content.

Content creators keyword-stuff their blog posts to please Google's algorithm.

Five

Solo thought leaders create intellectual property (e.g. books) out of their frameworks.

Content creators ghostwrite guest blogs to get a few backlinks.

Solo thought leaders innovate. Content creators copy Neil Patel.

You are working hard to create content and grow your business, so make sure you are focusing on the long game and not just the quick wins.

Are you developing thought leadership or just offering content marketing?

In the following pages, I will guide you through the process of becoming a solo thought leader and not just a content creator.

In *Making Money is Killing Your Business*, Chuck Blakeman uses the analogy of a treadmill to describe business owners who get stuck in the urgent things and have no time to take care of the important things that will grow their businesses. [5]

I believe it's the same with traditional content marketing. We can run on a treadmill, getting tired doing a bunch of stuff but not going anywhere. Or, we can get off the treadmill and take the exciting path to becoming solo thought leaders.

Checklist

☑ I have stopped obsessing over vanity metrics like post views, likes, and website visits.

☑ I have changed my mindset about content marketing and SEO.

☑ I have decided to become a solo thought leader and grow my business exponentially.

STEP 1
THE SOLO EXPERT

Become an expert in your niche

Chapter 3

Type "LinkedIn expert" in Google and the name Viveka von Rosen will come up in the top three results.

There may be hundreds of people claiming to be experts on LinkedIn, but Viveka is arguably the first one. Even her LinkedIn URL says it:

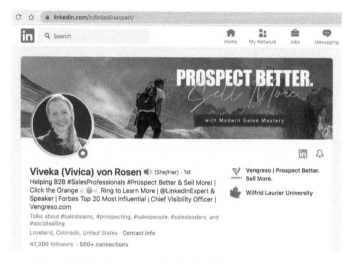

How did she become the LinkedIn Expert?

"It was a little bit of timing, a little bit of luck, and a little bit of synchronicity," she says. "Timing because I was fortunate—I got introduced to LinkedIn really early. There were not a lot of people teaching and training on it and certainly not a lot of women." [1]

One of the things to do when you're positioning yourself as an expert is finding a field or industry where you can stand out, either because it's a new field or you are unique in that industry. For Viveka, it was both. She saw the opportunity and jumped on it.

"The second thing was luck. Getting the social handles of @LinkedInExpert on LinkedIn, YouTube, and Twitter, was really big for a while. They helped establish my brand, even if I didn't have the social proof yet."

Viveka began blogging about LinkedIn in 2006, when very few people were writing about it. "That's how I got my first book deal. Wiley was looking for someone to write a book for them. I was not only blogging about LinkedIn, but I was putting my blog on my LinkedIn profile, so they were able to see that and then they reached out to me and I ended up writing, *LinkedIn Marketing: An Hour a Day.*"

I met Viveka while working at Vengreso, a sales training company she had co-founded with other sales thought leaders in 2017, and which now trains sales teams all over the world on how to sell with LinkedIn and use video for sales.

Her journey is similar to that of many aspiring solo thought leaders. Back in 2000, she had started a co-shared space. Then in 2005, she heard about LinkedIn. She rapidly became an expert and started teaching and writing about LinkedIn in 2006. The following year she felt ready to quit the co-shared space and went full-time into her consulting with LinkedIntoBusiness.

Viveka identified a niche, saw the potential for growth and became the go-to expert.

"A lot of my colleagues and competitors, who are no longer around, kept jumping on the latest and greatest thing, but I stuck with LinkedIn, although it was kind of boring at times. You must have the ability to find something that's new, unique, and opportunistic, and then, once you find it, not getting distracted by all the shiny objects. Stick with it if you can, because if you keep jumping down different lanes, you're never going to go anywhere. So, you need to be able to identify what's new, what's unique, where an opportunity is, and then you have to have the stick-to-itiveness."

Start by Defining Your Niche

In the previous chapter we talked about the concept of the Hedgehog. Your hedgehog is not a definition of who you are. It is about defining who you serve and how well you serve them. Having a hedgehog requires a narrow definition of your customer base.

Some examples of good hedgehogs are:

- A leadership coach who specializes in servant leadership.
- An attorney who only represents women going through divorce.
- A consultant who only works with SaaS companies with more than $10 million in revenue.
- A photographer who specializes in pets.

Many business owners are afraid that narrowing their customer base like this is leaving money on the table. But defining a customer base that has the ability to drive your economic engine, is what makes the difference.

Most people are more concerned about losing what they do not have than about taking care of what is already in front of them.

So, what is in front of you? Take a look at the market and figure out where the gaps are. That's what Marcus Chan did.

Marcus was a successful sales leader with proven results in Fortune 500 companies, who one day realized he could do better as his own boss and became a solopreneur. He observed that most sales coaches and trainers were going after the big fish—the high-ticket contracts to train the sales teams at large enterprises.

From his days as a sales professional, he knew that those training programs were usually outdated, cost a lot of money, and had no real impact.

"In those trainings," he says, "10% of people would do exactly as trained and get amazing results; 20% of people would be highly engaged in the whole training, but then they may not take action; and the other 70% were there because they were supposed to be there." [2]

So, Marcus decided to go directly to the sales reps instead of the companies. He knew that salespeople who looked for training and coaching outside of what their companies offered, were highly motivated and had a greater chance of success.

"Only a small percentage of people are actually willing to take action and get outside help," Marcus says. "So, I wanted to capture that market. I could cut through the noise by focusing on them because everyone else was focused on the companies. So I'm like, I'm gonna go toward the reps."

That's his hedgehog. He is not trying to reach everybody, just a segment.

If you are running a business that is trying to be everything to everyone then you have turned your business into a commodity. In this case, all you have to differentiate yourself is price. And there will always be someone who can beat you on price. Think about Walmart!

A great hedgehog will make you different from everybody else. It will give a clear handle for your strategic partners to carry you around and send you referrals. It will get you above the noise and you will be known as the expert in something.

Years ago, before LinkedIn became popular, I used to attend networking events in my town. You would go around the room with your stack of business cards, make a bit of small talk and hand over your card before moving to the next person. The funny thing is that 80% of the attendees were either realtors or financial planners.

They would introduce themselves like this: "Hello, I'm Susan, and I'm a realtor." Then the next person says, "Hi, I'm Tom, and I'm a realtor."

After the meeting, nobody remembers them, because they don't have a hedgehog. They are plain vanilla realtors.

I first learned about the hedgehog strategy while working as a business consultant with the Crankset Group. One of my favorite stories is about a Crankset client who started applying the hedgehog strategy in his business.

Mark (not his real name) was a realtor with a passion for cars. He had an unforgettable introduction: "I sell garages with attached houses for people who love cars."

Mark's website displayed photos of multiple-bay garages with luxurious sports cars in them. And on one corner, there was a small link that said, "Click Here to See Attached Home."

As a result, Mark more than tripled his income and became a hugely successful business owner. And the secret was narrowing down his market in such a way that he eliminated 99% of his potential market as a realtor.

Note that picking a niche doesn't mean going into an unknown industry or a very small market. Remember that one of the elements of a good hedgehog is that you should be able to make good money from it.

In the realtor's example, there is a lot of competition in the broad real estate industry, but Mark knew he could make more money by picking a sub-niche within that industry.

In other words, competition is a good sign that there is money to be made in a particular industry.

When you decide to go out into the world and become an expert, you are setting yourself against professionals around the world, all competing for the attention of your potential clients. That's why you must find your hedgehog.

A hedgehog that differentiates you from everybody else will wash away any fear of competition.

For instance, Viveka von Rosen says she is not concerned about all the LinkedIn experts popping up every day. "There's now 800 million users on LinkedIn. There's enough work out there for all of us, and so by picking your niche and focusing on that niche and being true to your message, you'll be successful. Don't worry about what's going on out there. Don't let that distract you. Competitors come and go. There's four or five of us, we all know each other, and we've been doing the same thing for a long time. But everybody else has come and gone. And the other thing is we don't all serve the same audience, so I'm not worried about it."

If you're clear about what you do, what your brand is and what your message is, your business will grow. But if you're always trying to change your brand, your message and your work to match something else, people will see through that, and you'll never be a solo thought leader.

How to Become an Expert

I lived in Toronto for only one year. Without work and struggling to grow my consulting business in a new (and very expensive) city, I had to make a decision. We had to make a change.

So, after more than a decade in North America, I moved my family to my hometown in Medellin, Colombia. The cost of living was much less expensive and we had a place to stay for free (my parent's home). But I had to find something to do.

What if I could somehow use everything I had learned in the U.S. and Canada and apply it to the local context?

Business practices were different in North America and what I told my clients in Canada was not always applicable to the average Colombian business owner.

Meeting others in our church I realized how young people struggled to find purpose in life, so I came up with the idea of applying business strategies to one's personal life.

I'd found my hedgehog. But I had to establish myself as an expert. And the first thing I needed to do was to become a student again.

Become a Student

I don't mean going back to school. If your industry requires a degree for credibility, then consider it. But there are many other ways to get an education.

As I founded the Vision and Leadership Institute, I began reading all the books by John Maxwell, the leadership guru in the West. I took extensive notes and shared my discoveries with others, both in writing and teaching.

In Decoding Greatness: How the Best in the World Reverse Engineer Success, Ron Friedman argues that the way to mastery starts with emulating existing experts and reverse engineering their methods.

You don't have to reinvent the wheel, only copy and improve. That is the natural way humans learn, like children imitating the sounds of adults around them to learn how to talk.

Tony Robbins says something similar. He insists that you should find someone who has already accomplished what you want to accomplish and ask them how they did it. [3] And if you can't ask them directly, at least read everything they wrote, attend their events and watch their videos.

Read everything from the top expert in your niche. Then read widely, take a class, or an online course.

"In a world where expertise is a moving target," Friedman writes, "the ongoing pursuit of knowledge is imperative to getting ahead. Staying on top of new innovations and professional trends is no longer just for go-getters—it's a basic requirement for staying relevant." [4]

However, don't stop at studying. Practice what you read and put your spin on it. There must be a moment when you stop reading and studying and start practicing.

"There are two things you can do to get better," says former tech executive turned solopreneur, Justin Welsh. "The first thing is you can read a lot and study a lot. And the second part is doing. Most people spend a lot of time studying as an excuse not to get started or they never study at all and they just get started and they don't know what they're doing. So, I think that there's a balance between those things." [5]

Unlike me, who decided to read tons of books, Welsh picked one book for each of the two areas he wanted to improve on: branding and copywriting.

"I just picked a book that got good reviews and I started reading it," Justin says. "And as soon as I felt like I understood the concepts well enough, I started trying. And trying is where I learned the most. Once you get started, you start to recognize where you're actually not very good. Then you keep studying and trying. I recommend that you pick someone that you enjoy and study their craft. And once you feel like you understand the basic concepts, the next thing to do is to get started."

This is good advice. Don't overstudy. If you only fill your head with information, you could end up being a clone, or unintentionally plagiarizing. Or even worse, you can become so impressed with what others are saying that imposter syndrome will creep in and paralyze you.

Find a Mentor from Whom You Can Learn

A mentor is someone with more experience and wisdom who can teach, guide, and encourage you to become a thought leader.

"I would not be where I am today if it wasn't for people like Bob Burg and Mari Smith," says Viveka. "Bob Burg was the walking-talking epitome of everything I wanted to be in business and then I actually met him through social media and we became really good friends. He became a mentor to me."

John Maxwell recommends that when looking for a mentor you start closer to home with family and friends. Perhaps they are not experts in your field, but you could learn about character, leadership, and business acumen. [6]

Then reach out to people you admire and ask them if they are willing to mentor you.

"Just find someone and reach out to them," says Viveka. "If they've got time, they'll mentor you; if they don't, they won't. I remember I was sitting in my office for the co-shared space and I wrote on Twitter: 'Does anyone know if Bob Burg is on Twitter?' And Bob himself DM me and said 'Yeah, I am.' I said, 'Oh my God, can I interview you?' And that's how it all began."

Once you find someone who agrees to mentor you, develop a plan and be prepared. The following are some best practices.

1. Plan your meetings.
How often are you going to meet and for how long? What do you expect to get from each session?

Come to each meeting with specific questions and take notes. Even better, record your sessions.

Remember that your goal is to become a thought leader, so you want to learn both about the topic and their journey to the top, both the content and the process. For example, there are some questions that will help you gain insights on their journey:

- Are there any mistakes that you made that I should be aware of?
- How did you become an expert? What resources did you use?
- How did you keep a tab on your progress?

Process questions focus on the execution:

- Tell me about your process. Where do you start? What are the steps you take?

- How do you plan?
- How do you come up with ideas, strategies, and tactics?
- Are there any disciplines that are helpful for you?

2. Do your homework.
Read your mentor's books and blog posts. Learn as much as you can about their thought leadership beforehand so you can ask deeper questions and not basic information already available online. That way you'll maximize your time and learn even more.

3. Execute what they tell you.
And finally, don't ask a thought leader to mentor you if you are not willing to follow their advice.

"If you're going to pick someone's brain," says Viveka, "be respectful of their time and, please, be accountable, follow-up. Do the work. Otherwise, you're just wasting everybody's time. I have done hundreds of calls. I've been a one-off mentor to hundreds of people who have asked for my time to pick my brain or whatever and only a fraction of them have ever followed up. So be respectful, please."

Bounce off Your Ideas with Others

My wife and I came up with an innovative teaching methodology while eating ice cream.

We were talking about her dream of starting an alternative education school while walking on a Saturday afternoon. We had just seen a property for sale and were imagining several groups of buildings connected by narrow walking paths.

"Like villages," she said.

"Yes," I said. "And each can be focused on a different area of knowledge."

That's how we came up with the T.E.A.M. pedagogy, which stands for Technology, Entrepreneurship, Arts, Mindfulness.

We didn't end up buying that property but the concept stuck and the TEAM methodology evolved into what is now an e-school with students across Latin America.

Bouncing ideas off each other has reaped amazing business results for both of us.

However, not all solopreneurs have a partner or close friend who can spur their thought leadership. That's why you should build a network of peers to bounce off new ideas. Intentional conversations can lead to new associations or connections, leading to a shift in your point of view about a certain topic.

Learn to think out loud with others, but not with just anyone. Well intentioned family members can kill your ideas with their worries and concerns. After all, if what they say is true, you are the average of the people with whom you hang out the most.

With this in mind, consider joining a mastermind group.

A mastermind is a group of five or six peers who meet in-person or online to give each other advice and support. You will give and receive advice about personal and pro-fessional issues, and brainstorm and learn with others.

"Do not try and go it alone," says Viveka. "Whether you pay for a mastermind or you create your own, that support is absolutely essential. I have a couple of different mastermind groups with some other LinkedIn experts and because we're in our own spaces, we don't overlap a lot. We can support each other without feeling competitive and needy. And I also have a network of women sales professionals."

If you're going to create your own mastermind, you must be unwaveringly accountable to each other because it's too easy to drop the ball when it gets hard. That's why paid masterminds do better because you put all this money in, so you're going to show up no matter what.

How do you find a mastermind group?

Ask successful people in your network, those you want to emulate, to see if they can recommend a mastermind.

Post the question on LinkedIn or Twitter such as, " What Mastermind has made the biggest difference to you? You'll probably get lots of input and then it's just a matter of finding the best one for you.

Search on Google or Meetup.com for mastermind groups near you, if you want to attend an in-person mastermind.

Get a Job

This may sound like an unpopular opinion. You are a solopreneur, after all, you are independent, so why would you want to get a J.O.B.?

Depending on what you want to be an expert at, sometimes working for a company in your field is the best way to learn a craft. Think about it like going to school but getting paid for it. Every year you spend at a company is like an MBA.

Megan Bowen says she values the 15-year career she had before partnering up with Chris Walker to build Refine Labs from scratch. "Don't knock the experience that you might have in a traditional job," she says. "All that experience has given me subject matter expertise. I definitely think young solo-preneurs can get started on their own, but there is definitely a benefit for working at a company, working for somebody else, and gaining experience figuring out what you like, what you don't like, seeing things that you want to do and things that you don't want to do, to help you clarify what you stand for and what you're offering."

This strategy won't apply to everyone, but it may work for you.

I've been an employee and a solopreneur on and off in the past decade, using my time within a company to acquire new skills and experiences, establishing relationships and industry contacts. In 2021, for instance, I was working for a SaaS company as a Content Marketing Manager, finding ways to apply thought leadership principles to the B2B space and learning from others in the company.

In fact, most of the solopreneurs and thought leaders I've interviewed for this book have a corporate background. Some of them were burned out after years of grueling work, others were laid off and others simply decided they would be happier working on their own.

Become an Expert, Not a Specialist

An expert knows everything in her field, plus more. The specialist knows everything in his field, but nothing else.

In other words, learn as much as you can about your niche, but keep broad interests. That's the way to be creative and leave a legacy.

In *Range: How Generalists Triumph in a Specialized World*, David Epstein says that nationally recognized scientists are much more likely than other scientists to be musicians, sculptors, painters, printmakers, woodworkers, mechanics, electronics tinkerers, glassblowers, poets, or writers, of both fiction and nonfiction. And compared to other scientists, Nobel prize winners are at least twenty-two times more likely to be amateur actors, dancers, or magicians.

In other words, they have range. These scientists "drew on outside experiences and analogies to interrupt their inclination toward a previous solution that may no longer work," Epstein writes. "Their skill was in avoiding the same old patterns. In the wicked world, with ill-defined challenges and few rigid rules, range can be a life hack." [7]

On the other hand, studies of specialist scientists and engineers concluded that those who did not make a creative contribution to their field lacked artistic interests outside their specialization. So, rather than focusing on one side of your brain, cultivate both.

Even those who specialize in the arts may suffer from rigid study and no range. Epstein also tells about Leon Fleisher, who was regarded as one of the great classical pianists of the twentieth century. Fleisher said that his "greatest wish" was to be able to improvise, because after a lifetime of masterfully interpreting notes on a page, he could not improvise at all. [8]

Here's my suggested action plan to becoming a solo expert:

- Set learning goals: What do you want to learn? When will you learn it by?
- Dedicate 90 to 120 minutes of uninterrupted concentration to carry out your learning plan everyday: Push yourself to learn something that challenges your mind and makes you feel outside of your comfort zone.

- Spend 25 minutes everyday reading, listening, or watching something outside your field.

And remember that it's okay to read the books, consume the blogs and the podcasts, watch the videos, and gorge on information if you like. But also do your own thinking.

Not just aloud with your mastermind group, but in deep thought and in your journal or notes. Because to become a solo thought leader is not enough to be an expert in what others have said. You must also develop a unique angle or point of view for your message. But that is the topic of the next chapter.

Checklist
- ☑ I am a student of my topic of expertise.
- ☑ I am always reading a book on the topic.
- ☑ I am always listening to podcasts or watching videos about my main interest.
- ☑ I am taking classes or online courses to gain new skills in my business.
- ☑ I have a mentor or am actively looking for one.
- ☑ I have a network of peers to bounce off ideas.
- ☑ I have joined or plan to join a mastermind group.
- ☑ I cultivate broad interests and have an artistic hobby or something outside my field.

STEP 2
THE SOLO INNOVATOR

Develop an innovative angle for your message

Chapter 4

David Meerman Scott says he is always trying to be aware of unusual patterns in the universe, things that other people don't see or at least are not talking about.

"When I see something that I feel is really interesting, I begin to write about it, typically on social media, on my blog. I might talk about it in a presentation and so on, because I'm kind of exploring the idea that I see. And if that generates interest from people, then I start to think if I have more to offer around this pattern in the universe. And that might lead to a book." [1]

The first time that David noticed some patterns in the universe that no one else was seeing was nearly 20 years ago. Everybody in the marketing world was talking about online marketing as an advertising channel—buying banner ads, renting email lists.

"This was pre social media," he says, "but I was seeing something completely different from everybody else. What I was seeing was that marketing on the web was really about creating content."

He began exploring those ideas and in 2005 published his first book, *Cashing In with Content*. The book didn't do too well, but in 2007, he wrote a book called *The New Rules of Marketing and PR*, which was one of the first books that talked about inbound marketing or content marketing.

The New Rules of Marketing and PR became a best-seller, it's now in its 8th edition, and has been translated into 29 languages.

Here's a summary of his approach:

- Look for trends no one else is writing about.
- Explore the idea while writing or speaking about it to your audience.
- Gauge interest in the idea based on the response.
- Develop the idea further into a system or process.
- Publish your system in a book.

In this chapter, we'll explore how to be unique and innovative so we can stand out as solopreneurs.

Being Unique

Solo thought leaders are not parrots. They don't repeat what everybody else is saying. They have unique points of view.

If you want to become a solo thought leader, you must not only have a vision; but be a visionary.

A visionary is someone with a larger-than-life vision of the future. She doesn't just dream, but dreams big. Just like the inventors of the hot air balloon or the airplane, they're usually ahead of their time and do something that hasn't been done before.

It's said that if Henry Ford had asked people what they wanted, they would have said faster horses; but he gave them the automobile instead, something that didn't even exist in the minds of people. The same happened with other great inventors such as Thomas Edison and even Steve Jobs.

Maybe you're not an inventor or a genius scientist, but you can find something different to innovate in your area of expertise.

Many years ago, while working as a medical writer at the University of Texas, I discovered a niche market in my own industry and found a way to profit from it. There weren't many ways to break into medical writing, other than having an advanced degree like mine, so in 2007 I wrote an ebook called *Becoming a Medical Writer: How to Launch a Successful Career Writing about Medicine and Health.*

At the time ebooks were something new, so I built a website and sold the 120-page PDF for $29.00. It was a hit and readers began asking for more information. So, I took some of the topics from the ebook and turned them into online courses, which I sold for a few hundred bucks each. In a couple of years I was earning more than $30K in passive income from this business. When the market was reaching a peak and Amazon released Kindle ebooks for less than $9.99, my sales began to decline—so I sold the business.

It wasn't an invention that transformed the world, but it was a profitable lesson, as I saw an opportunity in the new trend from ebooks to create an online business. You can do the same.

My wife loves to talk to children and she usually engages with them at the mall or the street. One particular thing she does instead of asking them, "What do you want to be when you grow up?" she asks, "What problem are you going to solve when you grow up?"

That's the question I want to ask you regarding your dreams. What problem of humanity are you going to solve?

Remember this:

Copycats are doomed to oblivion. Originals are doomed to succeed.

Innovate or die.

What is innovation?

Innovation has become a ubiquitous word nowadays in companies' mission statements. But what does innovation really mean? Is it just introducing changes or novelties to existing products? I believe it's more than that.

Innovation is doing something radically different from what everyone else is doing. Companies that experience massive growth and transform industries and societies are those that make things differently.

These companies seek to generate new demand or expand their markets instead of fighting with the competition for an existing market share. Their products are magnetic and people can't stop talking about them because they capture their imagination and provide inspiration.

The difference lies in their focus. These companies don't just try to gradually improve an existing product (like a smartphone with more megapixels); they don't settle with listening to their customers and adding the features they ask for.

These companies inspire and surprise their clients, giving them more than what they dreamed was possible.

These companies do not compete with others but focus on doing what they do with excellence, ten times better than anybody else, until their competitors seem infinitely inferior. In fact, they go beyond improving a product and focus on improving the future by transforming their industries. This is the case of Apple with the iPod and iTunes, transforming the music industry.

"There are two ways to become a music artist in the rock and roll world," David says. "One is to create original music and record and play your original music at concerts. Another way is to become a cover band and play other people's music. Nothing wrong with either of them. But a cover band can only get so far. It's very difficult to truly break out and make a lot of money if you're simply playing other people's music. However, if you're playing your own music, it's still hard to break out, of course, but ultimately you have an opportunity to change the world if your music becomes popular. The same thing is true of thought leadership."

David Meerman Scott's career is a testament of the power of transforming ideas, of looking for patterns that nobody else sees and writing about a very original concept before others write about it.

You can still make a decent living by taking other people's ideas and simply changing them a little bit, but that's not really becoming a solo thought leader.

How can you find those transforming ideas that will make you stand out as a solopreneur?

It all starts with an innovation mindset—a mindset that leads to wanting to find significant solutions that impact the world instead of just making money selling gadgets.

It's said that when Google founders, Larry Page and Sergey Brin, began working on their search engine, they told themselves that their product would change the world. And they did. The world wouldn't be what it is today (for better or for worse) without Google's legacy.

In fact, look at this quote by Larry Page during a speech at Singularity University in 2008: "I now have a very simple metric I use: are you working on something that can change the world? Yes or no? The answer for 99.99999 percent of people is 'no.' I think we need to be training people on how to change the world. Obviously, technologies are the way to do that. That's what we've seen in the past; that's what drove all the change." [2]

An entrepreneur with an innovation mindset will create solutions that are radically (10x) better for every process in his business (marketing, sales, management) and not only in the definition of the product or the vision of the company.

Not long ago, I read an article by an Airbnb former employee in which he praised that company's innovation culture. He tells of a time when he overheard one of the founders talking to a web designer back in the early days and telling him to create a website as the internet had never seen before.

That vision of being different and making an impact permeates everything that Airbnb does, even its website. It's no wonder that Airbnb is a threat to the hotel industry.

This mindset is not the result of luck or inspiration. It requires using creative methods for idea generation.

Coining New Concepts

David Meerman Scott popularized the concept of newsjacking, which later became listed in the Oxford English Dictionary.

Newsjacking is taking what's going on in the news and tying it back to your brand, either by creating real-time content or creating a product or service.

"I was thinking about newsjacking and although other people had talked about it, no one had really named it before. It was originally used in the 1970s in the UK to describe how people would steal newspapers from outside of a newsstand and then go sell them on a street corner."

David took the word and gave it a different meaning.

Years later, he popularized another concept, Fanocracy, which means turning fans into customers and customers into fans. According to David, fanocracy is when an organization puts the needs and wishes of fans ahead of every other priority.

"Fanocracy had been used a tiny bit before I used it. It was the name of a podcast at one point that had like six episodes and then folded. So, I wasn't the first person to use the word, but I was the first person to use it in a big way."

He published a book with that title and bought the URL. Now, whenever someone searches for newsjacking or fanocracy, they will find David Meerman Scott.

That's thought leadership.

How to Develop Innovative Ideas

We can all innovate. We just need to think out of the ordinary and be creative.

To get started, get away from the daily grind. David says he is always trying to clear his mind, looking for things that are not related to his work, reading about different topics, surfing, mountain biking, or hiking.

"That helps me to think of those patterns in the universe," David says, "because I'm not digging in and researching what other people have done in marketing. In fact, I think that would be counterproductive. I very rarely read other marketing books except for Seth Godin. I read everything he writes. But I don't really read very many marketing books because I don't want to focus on what other so-called marketing experts are talking about. I want to think of my own ideas. And I find that I come up with better ideas when I am in worlds outside of marketing."

One such world is music. David co-wrote a book with Brian Halligan, the CEO of HubSpot, and Bill Walton, an NBA Hall of Famer, called *Marketing Lessons from the Grateful Dead*.

They noted that The Grateful Dead became super popular partly because unlike every other band in the world in the 1980s, they were allowing fans to bring recording gear into their concerts and record shows.

"As a result people had these cassette tapes and later on MP3 files of these shows that they could listen to for free and The Grateful Dead weren't getting any money from that directly. But indirectly it was building a fanbase."

Now, here are some practical exercises to kindle your creativity.

Let your creative juices flow with brainstorming

Thomas Edison's notebooks were filled with crazy invention ideas. One entry from January 3rd, 1888, had more than a hundred ideas: a snow compressor, artificial silk, synthetic ivory, and an electric piano among other ideas. [3]

Uncensored brainstorming is useful to silence the inner critic and connect our brain to creativity. It helps us discover our passions because when we do it for a while, patterns emerge. You may discover a passion outside your profession or known abilities. That's good. Many successful companies were founded by people who knew nothing about their industry.

In fact, not having lots of inside information was an advantage because they came up with original ideas without anyone telling them it couldn't be done.

Airbnb's history is a great illustration. Brian Chesky and Joe Gebbia had no previous experience in the hospitality industry but now they're a giant of that industry. And it all started with an idea to make a few extra bucks.

When brainstorming, come up with as many ideas as you can. Quantity will eventually lead to quality.

Try this exercise: Take a blank sheet of paper and write between 30 and 50 ideas of a business you could start this week or a new product or service for your existing business. Don't overthink it and don't analyze whether it's feasible or not. They can be generic ideas, not necessarily detailed descriptions.

For instance, you can start with a list of areas you want to explore: an educational app, a healthy food service, crafts, online courses, something with animals, extreme sports, etc. Just let your creativity loose.

In fact, this is a simple hack I use to upgrade my business and my life on a regular basis. Every morning, before work, I have a quiet moment to think and write down 10 ideas to grow personally and another 10 ideas to grow professionally. It's a brainstorming session with no bad ideas. I know some will pan out, and others won't, but I'm just exercising my mind to see opportunities for growth.

We talk a lot about a bias toward action and execution. But without a constant flow of ideas, there's nothing to execute on.

Solve problems in a new way

It's said that Facebook was created because Mark Zuckerberg couldn't get a date. He had a problem finding a date so he created the student directory of his university to compare girls.

Just becoming aware of the daily problems around you can generate innovative ideas. Ask yourself all the time, what's the problem here? Then find a solution.

Once you become used to thinking in terms of solutions, start thinking outside your daily routines and instead think about ideas of global impact and long-term solutions. That's from where really innovative ideas come.

Megan Bowen says that when she faces a problem, she doesn't rely solely on her previous experience, but looks for three different ways to achieve her goal.

"There's many different paths to get to an outcome," she says. "So, I take a blank sheet of paper and ask myself, 'If there were no constraints and I could do whatever I wanted, what would I do?' Challenging yourself to come up with multiple paths to a goal, opens up and broadens your perspective and gives you a lot of different ideas to consider. Then you can evaluate what makes sense and what's feasible."

Now, let's look at six creative ways to solve problems.

1. Transfer solutions from one industry and apply them in another one, usually changing some elements.

Just like a hummingbird takes pollen from one flower to another, an entrepreneur can take solutions from one location to another.

In *The Creator's Code*, Amy Wilkinson tells the story of Howard Schultz, founder of Starbucks, who was inspired by the cafés he saw in Italy and took the concept to the United States. In fact, he began with an espresso bar called *Il Giornale*, with formally dressed waiters and opera music playing in the background. Apparently, people in Seattle didn't like that, so he switched opera for jazz and added tables and chairs for people to work while they enjoyed their coffee. [4]

Identify a concept that works in one place and plug it in somewhere else. Examine why and how the concept worked originally and what things would make it work again.

Solopreneurs are doing this as they leave their jobs and start their own businesses. For example, Bob Goodwin had more than 20 years of experience in sales in the B2B world. One day, he decided to quit and launch Career Club, bringing proven sales methodologies and tools to the job search to help people find a career that matters to them.

He transferred what works in sales to people looking for a job. "I speak in alliteration," Bob says. "So as a salesperson, what's my product? What am I selling here? And what's the value proposition? What do we do differently than the other guys? I use the four Ps. So first, what's my product? It's me, right. The second P is the pitch. How do I go and talk about this? In a concise, compelling way to somebody. The third P is prospects. Where are my prospects? And that's the database of employers, obviously. And then the fourth P is the process to follow. Salespeople would say it's a numbers game and they've got the CRM, and they've got a quota and they know that if I make a thousand sales calls, they will have 100 appointments that will lead to 10 proposals, that will get them the two deals they need for this quarter. That's a process that works for your job search as well." [5]

2. Recognize gaps and fill them with what is lacking.

Try to see problems and design new products or services to satisfy unmet needs in the market. Instead of focusing on existing solutions, search for what's missing. Listen to the silence, pay attention to what others ignore—and when you become aware of something that's not working, ask why.

For example, John Arms and his business partner, Jason Voiovich, founded Voyageur University, to help employed professionals become independent. They realized that because of the Covid pandemic, there would be a greater need for fractional leaders.

"People are trying to rebuild their businesses and completely remodel how they work," John says. "They're trying to find a way to get that critical gear in their business without bringing in somebody full-time. So, let's say, you're an Operations person. You've had a full-time role in Operations with success over the years. Now there is a business that needs an operator but doesn't want to pay $250k a year for that operator. A Fractional Chief Operating Officer (COO) can come just for a fraction of the time and help that business." [6]

There's a supply and demand side to fractional leadership. The demand side is growing, but where do fractional leaders come from? Most executives are working full time.

That's where Voyageur University comes into play to fill the gap. They are training former executives who were either laid off or left their jobs for whatever reason, and turning them into Fractional Leaders, who can now work remotely for up to four different companies at the same time.

3. Mix existing concepts to obtain new and different results.
Not long ago my family was hooked on a Netflix show. Each episode was a clever crash course on innovation. And it was a game show.

Baking Impossible pairs up bakers and engineers to design and bake creations that must survive intense engineering stress tests.

The judges assess the creations on three categories:

- Function (they must work)
- Design (they must be beautiful)
- Taste (they must be delicious)

Participants build edible robots made out of cake, rube goldberg machines out of desserts, sweet miniature golf courses, and more. And the technical term for this mix of disciplines is bakineering!

One of the best techniques for innovation and thought leadership is combining concepts from two different disciplines that at first glance have nothing in common, and come up with creative products.

How can you expose yourself to new disciplines? Here are some tips:

- Talk to experts in areas you don't know much about.
- Watch TED talks you wouldn't normally watch.
- Follow thought leaders outside your industry.
- Subscribe to weird podcasts.
- Read about history, science, art, gaming, AI...
- If your work is usually intellectual, take classes that require manual work or vice versa.
- Take on a creative hobby like drawing or painting.

4. Come up with new stuff by joining opposite concepts.
Have you ever wondered how glamping and luxury SUVs came to be? Someone had to mix the comforts of a five-star hotel and a luxury car, with the adventure of camping and carrying a lot of stuff in an SUV.

Try this exercise to get started: Find twenty problems

during the day without thinking about the solutions right away—they may be small or big problems.

If you have an existing business these can be: my customers are not aware of my services, my overhead costs are too high, people are not willing to pay what I charge for my service.

If you don't have a business, look for problems in everyday life such as bad breath, a dry mouth while you sleep, and having no time to buy groceries.

When you have the list with the twenty problems, start generating ideas. Bear in mind that there can be several solutions for one problem, or that one of the problems in your list can lead to other more interesting problems.

5. Question assumptions and reinvent a product.
Many times there's no innovation because we get used to the way things are, to the status quo. Innovation comes when we question widely-held beliefs about the world and the things around us and we begin to look at our surroundings with a new perspective.

For instance, when people questioned the basic assumptions about a chair—four legs, used to sit down—they came up with chairs with no legs, no backrest, standing chairs, and even uncomfortable chairs so people would not linger at fast-food restaurants.

Let's try a quick exercise. What are your assumptions about the following things?

- Social media posts
- Starting a business
- Creating an online course
- Writing a book

- Investing
- Getting a job
- Selling
- Marketing
- Coaching
- Consulting
- Leadership

You are probably copying what other successful people did, following a blueprint or a system. But what would happen if you turned those "tried and tested" methods upside down and do something unexpected?

Pick a product or service in an area that interests you and write down twenty assumptions about it. Then question those assumptions and create three business ideas inspired by the results.

6. Question your beliefs.
This goes beyond questioning assumptions.

I firmly believe in many things that are dead wrong. And so do you. How do I know that? Because I don't believe in everything I used to believe 10 years ago. Heck, even 1 year ago. So it's very likely that some of the things I believe today are wrong, too (I just don't know it yet).

With new information and exposure to other points of view, you change your mind, you refine your worldview, you abandon limiting beliefs and adopt a new mindset.

One of my favorite questions to ask myself is, "Why do I believe what I believe?" From religious dogmas to business practices, I question everything. It's one of the best ways to grow and reinvent yourself. You must question if the beliefs you've had until today have brought the results you really want. If not, go ahead and question them directly. Then teach others your discoveries.

One author who inspired me to question my beliefs was Vishen Lakhiani, the founder of Mindvalley.

In *The Code of the Extraordinary Mind*, Vishen says we must transcend our culture, questioning the Brules (bullshit rules) that are passed down generations and that hinder our growth and creativity. These rules make us ordinary and safe, not extraordinary and great. [7]

Vishen started questioning rules when he was a kid. He grew up in a Hindu family and was peeved at the rule of not being able to eat meat. He really wanted to try a McDonald's burger and asked his mother about it. He questioned the religious rule and insisted until his mother relented.

The burger wasn't as good as he had hoped, but he had created a new thinking pattern, a different neurological path in his brain that allowed him to innovate and build a successful business.

Run your ideas through a filter. Repeat the idea out loud several times and ask yourself honest questions like:

Do I really believe that? Why?
Do I want to be known for this?
Do these ideas add value to my niche or audience?

You must think bigger and in new directions. There is no other way if you want to become a solo thought leader.

Psychologists say we all suffer from confirmation bias, the tendency to latch on information that confirms our beliefs, and ignore or challenge any information that goes against them.

One thing that helps me fight confirmation bias is to intentionally look for and read authors with an opposite point of view to mine.

Sometimes those readings change my mind, sometimes they just enrich my point of view. For this book, for example, I looked for books that took a different angle on becoming an expert in your niche, and that's how I came across the concept of "range" and the importance of learning about topics outside your field.

Once you have questioned your beliefs and developed an angle for your topic, you are ready to take a stand.

Take a Stand on Your Topic

If your message and opinions are pleasing everyone, then they're not unique at all. If you are not creating strong emotions with your writing, you are not taking a stand.

As I mentioned earlier in the book, while regular content creators (a.k.a. cover bands) are happy with copying popular writers and not making any waves, solo thought leaders are not afraid to take a stand.

In fact, taking a strong (even controversial opinion) is almost always essential to stand out and create a big following. Tim Ferris, for example, built a reputation with an extreme opinion: the 4-hour work week.

Justin Welsh says he starts by asking himself, "What are my strong opinions? What are the things that I strongly believe?"

For example, he strongly believes that with enough intelligence and hard work anyone can build an online business. He also believes that you're going to live a better life if you have more time to spend with your family and friends, and doing the things that are important to you instead of working 40 to 60 hours a week for someone else.

Not necessarily controversial, per se, but divisive for those who prefer the employed life.

"Those are my opinions," he says. "It's just how I feel. So that allows me to craft content that will go out and attract people who feel the same way. You have to be really intentional about what you say. You want to attract like-minded people and repel people that disagree with you. That's okay. Understanding who you are or what you want and what you believe in is what allows you to go out and create content. Once you do that, you have to be consistent with your message. For example, you won't see me one day saying, 'I think everyone should give entrepreneurship a try.' And then the next day say, 'You know, I think everyone should work for someone else.' That would be inconsistent with my message."

Here are some action steps to take a stand:

- Decide what is the problem you want to solve or the message for which you want to be known.
- Figure out where you disagree with the prevalent point of view about that problem or topic.

- Define what is your unique way to see those issues and how you would like to transform others' points of view.
- Write down your opinions and beliefs based on the previous points and craft a narrative or story around it.

Once you understand what your strong opinions are and deliver them consistently to the people that you want to attract, you can get them into your group of fans. When they start following you or reading your newsletter or watching your videos, you can deliver high-quality valuable content that keeps them growing with you. Soon you will have built a community around your thought leadership.

But beware that taking a stand will bring a lot of criticism and haters. That's why you should be prepared to deal with negativity.

Become Immune to Criticism

One of my writing mentors used to say that writers need to have a thick skin. When we work with editors, they provide constructive criticism and point out flaws in our writing. He was right, because my editors have deleted whole paragraphs and made edits mercilessly and crossed-out hundreds of words.

And that's before publishing the book. Afterward, a writer receives criticism from all those who didn't like the book. During my career I've written many articles and books on controversial topics that have brought both fans and haters.

My first novel, for example, deals with the history of geology and how modern geological theories originated out of political and religious views and not solely on science and research. Amazon reviews range from "the best book I've ever read" to "this is a piece of literary trash." I admit that at first I felt hurt by the bad reviews, but I shook it off and kept writing.

Back in 2008 I published a book about vaccine safety along with an M.D. and public health expert, which brought a huge backslash from anti-vaccine groups who accused us of ugly things.

Years later, I tackled another controversial issue, writing against the religious establishment and calling for a more genuine Christian faith, one not dependent on rituals, traditions, and titles. That brought on a lot of criticism as well, but I've developed immunity to this sort of negativity.

A solo thought leader must walk around with a "bulletproof vest" for protection against trolls, haters, and well-intentioned relatives. Many will tell you that you're crazy, that you're wrong, that what you do doesn't work. But you must understand that it's impossible to please everybody.

Critics often speak from their own fears and frustrations. They can't see what you can see; they don't have your perspective or your passion, so you must not listen to them.

While a mentor or mastermind group will correct you on the path to thought leadership because they have walked that same path before, a critic is someone who's never gone to where you're going, and won't even try it.

Just as you don't take financial advice from a guy who's broke, don't take the bad rap from someone who doesn't dare to dream as big as you do.

Once you have developed a unique angle for your message, you must also learn how to communicate it in a unique way. How? Finding your voice.

Checklist

☑ I am developing an innovation mindset, thinking of solutions no one has generated before.

☑ I am coming up with new ideas all the time through uncensored brainstorming, training my mind to see opportunities for growth.

☑ I am learning from other disciplines outside my expertise.

☑ I question my beliefs on a regular basis and listen to different opinions.

☑ I have taken a stand on the most important issues in my industry and can express my opinions clearly.

☑ I am developing immunity to criticism.

STEP 3
THE SOLO ARTIST

Find your unique voice

Chapter 5

Finding your voice is a common advice that always felt too abstract for me. Something reserved for artists or novelists.

In fact, I first heard the term when learning how to write fiction. Finding my literary voice sounded almost magical, like trying to emulate masters such as Gabriel Garcia Marquez or Hemingway. It seemed impossible.

But finding your voice is simpler than I thought. It's about writing or speaking in a way that is both comfortable for you and that resonates with your audience.

"When I was just getting started, I looked at attention as my friend," says Justin Welsh. "I wrote content every day before I even had a business, just to find my voice. I started on LinkedIn. I shared my thoughts and observations about many topics that I found interesting, and inside of all of that noise were some signals. Sometimes I bombed, sometimes I struck a chord. The more I looked at what resonated, the more I doubled down. This allowed me to understand what people cared about."

Finding your voice implies finding your medium of communication. Justin attracted attention through his writing, which is something he enjoys.

"I don't enjoy video. I don't enjoy audio. I don't do Instagram. I just wanted to write and my goal was to get a little bit of attention through writing and that writing was hopefully going to help some prospective clients find my business. And that worked."

Some gurus like Gary Vee insist that you should be on every social media platform, on every channel possible. That may be fine for a large team, but as a solopreneur, you are better off focusing on what you do best.

Test your ideas in different ways and channels until you find the one that works best for you. Whether it's writing or making videos, podcasting or blogging, you probably have one that you are better at and to which your audience responds better.

- Justin writes great LinkedIn and Twitter posts.
- Chris Walker has amassed a big following with his podcast State of Demand Gen, and short video clips on LinkedIn.
- David Meerman Scott's forté is writing best-selling books and public speaking.

Just because you can do many things well, it doesn't mean you should. I've done YouTube videos, podcasts, ebooks, public speaking, online courses, and more. What I do best, though, is writing. That's why instead of doing all of the above, I focus on writing long-form posts and a weekly newsletter. I love writing and my audience responds to that.

Once you find a medium and a channel, your voice will be sharpened by the response of your audience, both content and form.

For instance, Justin started writing about building SaaS sales teams, which was his background. That garnered some attention and built a following. But then something unexpected happened.

"People got really interested in the writing itself," Justin says. "How do you write? How do you attract people to follow you? How do you grow a social media following? That wasn't my intention when I started. The intention was to get clients. And so a year into my business, I started recognizing the opportunity to start helping people do what I was doing online, to start helping people write better, grow their social media following, build their own online business, become a consultant and advisor. I never thought I would be a social media person in that respect."

As you start communicating your message, gather all the feedback you can get, from questions to objections. These will help you hone and improve your messaging and refine your voice.

Assess your content with these questions:

- How do people react to my content?
- Are they excited, intrigued, inspired, or enraged?
- Do I clarify things for them or do I confuse them? (You can tell by their comments and questions.)
- What types of content resonate more with my readers/viewers and why?

Be careful though—sometimes you may get carried away from your niche and expertise if you use your content as a popularity contest. Let's say one day you decide to post on social media about something outside your niche, just for fun or because it is a trending topic. And let's say that your post goes viral.

What do you do next? Do you treat it as a one-off, an outlier among your regular posts? Or do you drop everything else and start pursuing this new topic on a daily basis?

If you want to become a solo thought leader, stick to your niche. Jumping on the bandwagon of popular topics will only hurt your credibility and keep you from making an impact.

Let me give you an example. I post daily on LinkedIn on two topics: thought leadership and writing. In fact, my newsletter is about writing like a thought leader. But on the weekends, I sometimes go a bit off topic and write some more inspirational, self-help type posts.

One of those weekend posts generated 10x more views than my average weekly post (see image below).

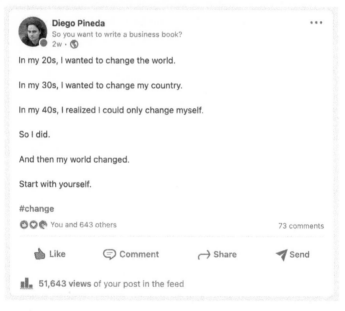

Of course, it would have been tempting to switch gears and ride that wave of popularity, writing inspiring haikus and personal development posts regularly. But as we heard from Viveka von Rosen in a previous chapter, one of the keys to becoming a thought leader is stick-to-itiveness.

The same temptation arises when you see the popularity of others. You may want to imitate their style, try to write like they write and speak like they do. But if that is not your personality or what you feel more comfortable with, that's all it would ever be: trying.

"If you're trying to mimic other people's voices, it's not true, it's not authentic," says Viveka. "It might work for 10 seconds, but it's not you. I think about those viral TikTok videos where people are singing other people's songs and it's like, okay, that's cool. They got millions of views but it's not their true voice. So, you've got to find your own voice and be consistent. In the past 17 years, you know, how I look, how I talk, what my product looks like... that's changed. It has to. But that voice, that core of your message, that needs to remain consistent."

What do you sound like?

Every person has a vocal timbre, a particular tone that gives personality and color to their speaking voice.

Your timbre is more recognizable when you are in a relaxed environment and you feel free to express yourself. For instance, if you are afraid of public speaking, your voice may sound robotic or muffled when in front of an audience.

The same can happen when you write. You may be so worried about the grammar and the structure of your content, that it feels rigid and boring. It can be grammatically correct, but it doesn't carry your voice.

Pay attention to what you sound like when you are among family and friends (record yourself if you like), without thinking about sounding smart or insightful.

Then take note of what is natural in your personality. Are you funny or serious? Long-winded or brief? Bold or reserved? Knowledgeable or inquisitive?

Then take the most positive traits of your personality and voice and incorporate them into your style, taking into account your audience's preferences.

If you are in the self-help industry, being funny and provocative works best. If you are into finances and business, being a straight talker works well.

Create your unique personality through your voice, adding elements that people will immediately recognize as yours.

Some thought leaders include self-deprecating humor or sarcasm in their writing. Others incorporate swearing into their speech as part of their voice, like Marie Forleo, Tony Robbins or Rob Moore, who use the f-word as often as any preposition.

However, this is not always gratuitous. There should be a reason behind your choice of style.

In a TV interview, Tony Robbins was asked why he used profanity during his seminars. This was his answer:

"I read a book at 22 years old called *Taboo Language*, which changed my life. It was written by a brilliant psychiatrist who had studied Freud. And he said that Freud was a genius and he was messed up. He was addicted to cocaine, he thought everybody wanted their mother. But his genius was that if you tried to make a change and you didn't succeed it was because consciously you said one thing and unconsciously another. And so he would use provocative language to disturb or jolt the person out of the surface bullshit to something deeper that was real. I use it and you see people get shocked or they laugh or whatever. And when they are shocked or they laugh, then what comes out is the real them instead of the manufactured how I think I should be. And then you can make real change, because what makes real change happen is getting real. You can't do it as long as you live in old patterns. Old patterns control us, so my goal is to help break through that." [1]

Great writers have a distinct style, like Cole Schafer, a copywriter whose irreverent newsletter is like a guilty pleasure. For example, an average writer would ask his subscribers, "Have you already bought my guide? Check it out here!"

But not Cole. Here's the same call-to-action in his words:

"Last night, I was thinking about how so much writing today doesn't 'finish strong' but instead dies slowly, miserably, like a week-old party balloon. So, I shared some candid thoughts on the subject in my guide. If you've already purchased the guide, then it's your fucking birthday. You've got lifetime access. Just log back in. If you haven't purchased the guide, shame on you. Write your wrongs here. Or, by tapping the big black button at the very end of this email."

As a solo thought leader you'd want to be recognized as someone who provides value, knows your stuff and is trustworthy and likable.

Whatever you decide, make sure that whenever someone visits your site or reads your posts or watches your videos, they'll know in an instant that they're in the right place.

Voice is Also Your Visual Brand

Another way to develop your voice is with a unique visual identity, from your logo and colors to your tagline.

Viveka's tagline, "The LinkedIn Expert" says it all, for example. Think of your tagline or headline as your personal mission statement. Avoid generic terms and use words that will resonate with your audience. Get creative but don't go over the top with a funny or cheesy statement (unless you're a comedian!). When people search for connections on LinkedIn, they'll see your headline and decide whether to click or even accept your connection request based on your headline. So, make it awesome.

"If you're really clear on what your message is," Viveka says, "your brand will spring from that and I mean, your whole brand, even your colors."

Viveka advises creating a well branded LinkedIn Profile, using a background image that speaks to who you help and how you help them and a headline (220 characters) that talks to your buyer specifically.

"I think a big mistake some people make is being too much of a generalist," she says. "And if you're trying to be all things to all people, you're going to be nothing to no one. So be very clear on that unique audience and speak only to them and let them know what you do because there's enough out there for everybody else."

John Arms told me about one of his clients who was trying to position himself as a fractional leader, but could not think of something that would differentiate from anyone else in his field (finance).

So John asked him: "What is it over the arc of your career that people have relied on for you that you're really, really good at and that you enjoy doing?"

His client, Doug, thought about it and said, "You know, I've always been the company's Fire Marshal. Like when everything is on hot, smokin fire with finance issues, I've always been great at putting those out."

That conversation led to a great branding discovery and "The Fire Marshall of Finances" became Doug's new headline. Unique, attractive, and full of possibilities.

Most LinkedIn profiles are devoid of a consistent branding. There are some great exceptions, though, like Michelle Griffin, a personal brand strategist, who uses bright colors in her branding to stand out. The background of her profile picture is yellow and her posts immediately jump out when someone is scrolling down their feed.

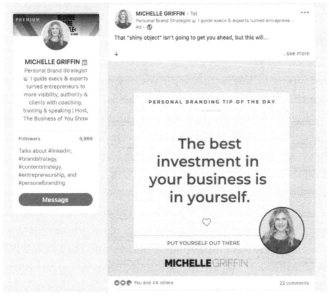

"Personal branding encompasses many aspects and visual identity is an important component," says Michelle. "On LinkedIn, I noticed very few entrepreneurs branding themselves with a stand-out consistent identity and color is one area where people resonate. I went with yellow to represent my brand. First, the yellow brand color I chose is the same hue as the universal smile emoji and also represents, being clear, positive, warm. That's the emotional connection I want others to impart from me: creative, happy, friendly, and encouraging. I use yellow in everything I do, from my profile picture, banner, post graphics, LinkedIn Live graphics, podcast cover art, you name it. And it's been a big part of my personal brand this year. I'm constantly getting DMs and comments on my "bright yellow" branding and yellow profile picture and banner. I should have started counting, but it's typically a few each week, so I know it's doing its job." [2]

Your Ideas Also Need a Style

Solo thought leaders change the way people think and behave with the power of words.

That's why you must use your words in a very strategic way. "Category Pirates" Eddie Yoon, Nicolas Cole, and Christopher Lochhead, call this "Languaging." Languaging is going beyond being better and being different; it's a line of demarcation between the old and the new.

They write: "When Henry Ford called the first vehicle a "horseless carriage," he was using language to get the customer to STOP, listen, and immediately understand the FROM-TO: the way the world was to the new and different way he wanted it to be. Had he called the first vehicle a "faster horse," that would have been lazy languaging (and lazy thinking)." [3]

Other examples of languaging in action are:

- Pfizer invented a new disease called "erectile dysfunction" and not "impotence."
- Netflix created "streaming" as a new way of watching movies.
- Starbucks coined *Grande, Venti*, and *Tall* as new ways of naming coffee sizes.

These are examples from big companies, but can solopreneurs design new categories and become industry leaders? Sure they can.

Let me introduce you to Jaime Jay, the co-founder of Bottleneck Distant Assistants.

Jaime's business was doing well until early 2020, providing Virtual Assistants to different clients. But when COVID-19 hit, he lost half of his clients.

"That was really tough," Jaime says. "I had to make a decision. Should I move forward? Should I close? What should I do?" [4]

With the help of Christopher Lochhead, they chose the much harder route of reimagining themselves and came up with a new category.

"So we reimagined what a virtual assistant is," Jaime says. "We jumped on the tail end of social distancing and the fact that people were working remotely and still being productive and didn't always have to be in an office environment. And because of that silver lining and Christopher's insight into reimagining our category, we created a brand new category called Distant Assistance. We've been able to thrive now and we've completely redone our infrastructure."

Coming up with a new category has allowed Jaime to find a voice and a style that sets him apart from all the companies offering virtual assistants.

It all starts with a provocative point of view (POV). Your POV will frame your customer's problem and your solution in a new way. According to the category pirates a POV is: "What do we stand for?"

Then comes Languaging, which is: "How do we powerfully communicate our POV?"

And that influences the messaging: "What should we say?"

Jaime's POV goes something like this:

The Problem: Many business leaders are doing the wrong things, instead of focusing on doing their best work. They are answering emails and phone calls, managing their calendar and other admin stuff, instead of creating partnerships, raising money and growing the business.

The Old Solution: Business leaders hire virtual assistants on Fiverr or other places to perform certain tasks, creating a transactional relationship.

The New Solution: A Dedicated Distant Assistant, who offers a more intimate relationship. A Distant Assistant is not just a contractor that completes a list of tasks. During the 90-day onboarding, she will discover your tone, your voice, learn your vision, your mission, your core values, and how you make decisions so they can make decisions on your behalf.

"They become a project manager and advocate," Jaime says. "They enjoy pursuing the vision that you pursue and pretty soon, before you know it, emails will be responded to in your voice and you'll be hard pressed to see the difference between an email that you send versus the email your distant assistant sends because now you're using the same vernacular, using the same words in the same tone."

The new Distant Assistance category has catapulted Jaime's business to new heights, although it's a new term with which people are unfamiliar.

"The trick behind creating a new category is that it's something that's not out there. But I would rather be a leader in an industry rather than a small fish in a big pond where everyone else is fighting for those magic words, 'virtual assistant'. I wanted to create my own."

In just 10 months, thanks to their marketing efforts, Distant Assistant has become a new buzz word in their industry. And because his company owns the category as the inventors of the term, it all leads to them.

Incorporating languaging into your business will elevate your ideas above your personality and even your branding, and make you a unique thought leader.

Or, in my own languaging: a Solo Thought Leader.

Once you find your voice and create a new category where you are the king or queen, you have to get the word out. How? Becoming a Solo Educator.

Checklist

☑ I have found my voice: I know my preferred method of communication and my audience responds to what I communicate.

☑ I know how to infuse my personality into my writing and speaking styles.

☑ I have developed a consistent visual brand for my website, social media profiles, and other assets.

☑ I am using languaging in my messages and frameworks to differentiate myself as a solo thought leader.

STEP 4
THE SOLO EDUCATOR

Educate your audience and dominate social media

Chapter 6

"Education doesn't need to be reformed, it needs to be transformed," said the late Sir Ken Robinson. [1]

That quote was the seed of an idea that made a homeschool mom start coaching other moms and later start an alternative education school in the mountains of Colombia.

Two years later, thanks to COVID, disrupting schools worldwide and a dose of innovative thinking, this solopreneur has expanded her school across Latin America and created a new category: the e-school.

Traditional education, especially in Latin America, is antiquated, still rooted in memorization of information that is easily accessible online and dominated by standardized tests. The pandemic moved everything to online classes for a while, but although the format changed, the contents were the same.

"An e-school is not simply a better online or virtual school," Diana says. "It's a flexible educational model where the student is at the center, not the teacher, nor the curriculum. We develop the talents of each student and teach them the skills they need for the 21st century. We are the first school to develop a curriculum for Gen Z, for native digitals."

Rhema e-School teaches kids from K to 12, non-traditional subjects like entrepreneurship, mindfulness, coding, graphic design, personal finances, trading, all types of arts, and more.

The response from students and parents has been unbelievable.

And I should know. Diana is my wife.

Innovating in education has not been easy, particularly when you are challenging the establishment. Diana has found resistance from government officials, public school teachers, and families who frown upon anyone disturbing the status quo.

"I've to become an educator not only for my students, who are my users," Diana says, "but for their parents and extended families, who are my clients. We developed a new teaching methodology and began to write blogs, make videos, infographics, and distribute them through social media. Actually, it all started when I made a video explaining my vision and it went viral on Facebook. That was my proof of concept, sort of."

Second to innovation, education is the most important duty of a solo thought leader. Without it, you are just an expert.

The solo educator leads through a well-thought-out system or framework that is communicated through multiple channels.

Jaime Jay says the trick of creating a new category is educating people about something that didn't exist before. The challenge is real because the new category is not a keyword phrase people are actually looking for in Google. It has no SEO value (yet).

"How do you educate people?" Jaime says. "You simply share your story, you talk about the journey. You start talking about distant assistance, you go to podcasts and you get interviewed in Forbes magazine and things like that. And the word eventually gets out. Just keep saying it, keep saying it. And then right when you think you're getting sick of it, say it more, just keep talking about it. That's it. Just keep pushing it out there, but don't trademark the category."

Although it may be tempting to trademark the category you just invented, it's not a good idea, because you might be cutting off the wings of your category. David Meerman Scott, for example, says that for newsjacking and fanocracy he bought the domains, but he didn't trademark the terms. [2]

"I did not try to claim ownership over newsjacking," he says. "I did not try to claim ownership over fanocracy. And by not claiming ownership over them, I basically said to the marketplace, 'If you want to write, speak, or do some work around newsjacking, go ahead.' In fact, there are a number of different public relations agencies that have a newsjacking practice. I don't get any royalties, they don't even mention my name, but that's cool because they're spreading the idea of newsjacking."

Become a Storyteller

"I've told my story hundreds of times," Diana says. "Whenever I talk to parents wanting to know more about the e-school, I tell them of my own journey, how our oldest son hated school and got himself kicked out. He had no interest in academic stuff, he just wanted to play music and make money. So, I homeschooled him and helped him learn to play instruments and taught him about entrepreneurship. The school wanted him to excel in math, science, and social studies, but his passions were music and business. And today, years later, he has his own company and his own band in which he plays the drums, the piano, and the guitar, and records his own music. That's why at Rhema e-School, we start by discovering what each student is passionate about and we help them develop their talents. That story really resonates with parents who see that their kids are frustrated with the one-size-fits-all approach of traditional schooling."

Your success as a solo thought leader depends on your ability to hone a compelling story of transformation and tell it to your audience. You'll need both your origin story (your "hero's journey") and, later, the story of your customers. People should be able to hear or read your story, how you overcame the odds against you, and be able to see themselves in that journey. That's how they'll relate to you and align with your message and point of view.

"Nobody has ever been in your shoes," says Jaime. "There's a lot of people like you or a lot of people doing maybe a similar thing, but never exactly. What's ordinary to you is extraordinary to someone else. And being able to share your experience creatively through storytelling will differentiate you. When you tell your story, other people resonate with that story and that is how you build your network."

Jaime tells his story at the beginning of his book to set the stage. He had just returned from being away with the U.S. Army to be with his family, when his wife told him she wanted a divorce. Not only that, but he could not go back to their home. He ended up homeless, without a job and with no family. Thanks to some friends, he was able to get a job at a restaurant, later he got a corporate job, and finally started a business and met his new wife. It's a story of facing uncertainty and making it through tribulations.

Storytelling is a superpower you must acquire as soon as possible. When I teach creative writing to the kids at Rhema e-school I use examples from their favorite movies. I'd like to do the same now to show you the elements of a great story.

Have you seen the Captain America movie?

If I asked you what the movie is about, you'd say something like this: "It's about a young guy called Steve Rogers, who wanted to enlist in the U.S. army, but he was skinny and weak. Until one day a scientist gave him a serum that turned him into a super soldier. With his super strength he was able to fight the Nazis in World War II."

The basic plotlines are:

- Introduce a character (Steve Rogers)
- Who has a goal (enlist in the army)
- But there were obstacles in his way (his physique)
- So, the character undertook a transformation (with the serum)
- That allowed him to accomplish his goal (fight the Nazis)

In other words, every story you tell must have certain elements to be compelling (and in a certain order). Here they are, illustrated with Jamie's story:

- A character (Jaime)
- A motivation or goal (Be with his family)
- A conflict or obstacle (His wife asked for a divorce)
- A character arc (from homeless to entrepreneur)
- A new reality (new family, new career)

Without character, there is no story; just random thoughts. Without conflict, there is no story; just an anecdote.

Movies and novels can get a bit more complex and include elements like a mentor or guide, a villain, a calling, and more. But the above are the basic ones you need to tell a great story.

Reflect on your own story and identify the elements of storytelling noted earlier. You can do the same for one or more of your clients (you may need to interview them).

The most important thing is to have a strong character arc. It can be a physical change like Steve Rogers' transformation, or it can be a change of character. For example (now that we are talking about superhero movies), think about Tony Stark (a.k.a. Iron Man). At the beginning of the saga, he was a selfish, rich brat. But he becomes a hero who sacrifices himself to save the universe (literally). Not all stories are heroic like Iron Man's or as dramatic as Jaime's, of course.

Justin Welsh says every solopreneur should have a "founder story" to use as a marketing asset, and he created a 7-step framework that anyone can use as a template to create their story.

1. The Obstacle
It's important that your audience can relate to your story, and there's one critical thing that's relatable to anyone: overcoming an obstacle.

Justin's obstacle: "I had gotten fired 3 times by the time I was 28 and was basically a failure heading into 2010."

2. The Internal Struggles
Show your audience how you felt inside because of the obstacle, with words like fearful, insecure, or worried.

Justin's internal struggle: "After getting fired 3 times, I was worried that I was never going to be successful at anything."

3. The External Struggles
These are struggles that can be seen or heard, like an over-drafted bank account, a lost job, or a poor living situation.

Justin's external struggle: "My buddies made fun of me for living in tiny towns and getting fired. A girlfriend even dumped me because I had too much debt."

4. The Change Event

This is the critical decision you made that leads you from your struggle to your newfound transformation.

Justin's change event: "I took a bus ride from Allentown, Pennsylvania, to New York City to interview at a small technology company called ZocDoc."

5. The Spark

The spark is that magic moment when you realize everything is about to change, when you went from feeling completely disconnected to reinvigorated.

Justin's spark: "When I started working at ZocDoc, I was sparked by the product, the people, and the energy of the city."

6. The Guide

The guide in the story is the person who lifts you up and helps you see your potential for what it really is.

Justin's guide: "After years of making no sales in my previous jobs, my boss went out with me on my first day and helped me make a sale."

7. The Result

The result is the continuation of the story to even greater success, leading up to your present situation.

Justin's result: "I never looked back. I got promoted multiple times and went on to become an executive at a startup company in LA at age 33."

Business leaders that have mastered the art of storytelling include Phil Knight, Richard Branson, and Brian Chesky. They've told the story of their companies and have captured the attention of many, who now retell their stories everywhere.

Telling a compelling story isn't just for startup founders, but for any solopreneur. So, tell stories worth retelling.

Captivate your readers with stories of transformation and results. That way, they'll believe that if it was possible for you (or your clients), it will be possible for them. Because your story can also be their story.

Do you need a website or a blog?

I created my first website in Geocities in 1998. If you remember Geocities, high-five fellow Gen-Xer!

I've created dozens of websites and blogs since then, so for me, the answer to this question is a no-brainer. But I've met many solopreneurs that in 2022 who don't have a website yet. They may think it's not worth it, or too hard, or that social media is enough (more about social media later).

But the data is clear: businesses with a blog get 55% more traffic than businesses without a blog. B2C companies report that having a blog increases sales opportunities by 88%. [3]

In case that's not enough, let me give you five reasons why solo thought leaders should have a blog to educate their audience.

1. Having a blog will allow people to find you.

If they search for your name or your category on Google, you want to make sure they find you. It doesn't matter if you don't own the most competitive keywords in your field, you will be found for your languaging magic, like David with fanocracy, or Jaime with distant assistance.

The more blog posts you publish about your topic, the greater the chances of being found.

2. A blog is a great way to showcase your expertise.

Which is the one place where you can frame your customer's problem and the solutions you offer? Your blog.

Unlike social media where people would need to infinitely scroll down to find all your topics, you can organize your blog posts in a way that makes the most sense.

A blog is low-cost marketing.

3. A blog is a conversation starter.

Although most people think of interacting with others through social media (and they are right), a blog can also become a place where you can create a community, where people can comment on your articles or videos, and you can answer their questions.

When you publish regularly, you can create an email list for people who want updates. And as you may already know, an email list is one of the most important assets in your business.

4. A blog allows you to express your voice and personality.

Since it's your own site and you don't have a word limit or editorial guidelines to follow, you are free to express your opinions and give your passionate voice free rein. Use your blog to let people know your human side and why you do what you do. Show them what happens behind the scenes.

5. A blog is the foundation for your content strategy.
When you write a good blog post, you can repurpose it in
many ways:

- Using excerpts for text posts on LinkedIn and
  Twitter
- Creating video versions for YouTube and TikTok
- Developing a podcast inspired by the blog post
- Creating infographics for Instagram
- Sharing the link on your newsletter
- Republishing the article on Medium.com

What makes a great thought leadership blog post?
Search online for "the anatomy of a great blog post" and you'll
find generic advice from HubSpot and the likes about the number
of words, the types of headlines and subtitles you should use,
the SEO elements you must include and the classic structure of
introduction, body, conclusion, and call to action.

They tell you to use attractive headlines like "The
Ultimate Guide to..." or "10 Proven Strategies for..." or "How
to Get Started with..."

But thought leadership doesn't really care about the rules
above. What then? Glad you asked. Here are my principles
for a great thought leadership blog post:

- Hook your readers with curiosity.
- Explain concepts with clarity.
- Write with emotion.
- Use the CPE method.

1. The hook

Have you ever been hooked on a television series? I have.

A full weekend binge-watching "Money Heist"? Yes, my wife and I have done that.

You know why? Because the writers of the series are brilliant, the actors are top notch and the story is gripping and addictive.

I bet you'd love people to binge on your blog posts, podcasts, videos, or whatever content you put out. But do they? Maybe they give you some likes, some comments, they open your emails (sometimes) and learn a thing or two.

But, do you want to know how to hook them on your content? I'll tell you in a minute.

You see, your audience craves entertainment. Actually, they crave the neurochemicals released into their system when their curiosity is triggered by the plot of a TV show: dopamine and norepinephrine.

Scientists say these neurochemicals are as addictive as cocaine. And that is good news for you as a blog writer.

Unless you are writing scripts or novels, you are not in the entertainment business. You want to help others, inspire them, educate them somehow. Not just entertain them, right? Still, you can use neurobiology to your advantage.

Want to know how? It's a simple technique I use in my novels. And I am using it here. A few paragraphs above, I promised to tell you how to hook your readers. But I haven't done it yet. I made you curious about something, then I withheld the information for a while.

That curiosity created a surge in your brain activity. Then I revealed the secret and your brain rewarded you with another neurochemical that makes you feel good.

(The dopamine levels here are not as high as with a story that involves more senses, but the principles are the same).

Let me tell you more. See what I just did?

I don't want you to stop reading just yet, so I make another promise and get you curious again. That's how a TV show or a book series can last for years. It creates questions in the audience, resolves some, but keeps stacking up more questions.

One season ends in a cliffhanger scene where you don't know whether the villain is dead or alive. You wait until next season to find out that he escaped at the last instant. But at the end of that season there is another cliffhanger.

In fact, there are cliffhangers before every commercial break and at the end of each episode (or book chapter). Why? To keep you hooked, wanting to come back for more. So, apply this principle to your blog posts.

2. Clear explanations

Last year we bought a condo, and had to sign a 100-page contract. And although I've read hundreds of books and articles, including medical journals, I could not understand that contract. If legalese is an official language, it should be illegal!

So, I met with the agent from the builder and asked him to explain clauses 2.1, 2.4, 3.6, and so on. He read and re-read the clauses, made some notes, frowned a few dozen times, and then tried to explain it.

It didn't match up.

"I understand you," I said. "But what you're saying is not what is written in here."

Can you relate? Obscure writing is like a venereal disease infecting all sorts of industries. The good news is that there is a treatment.

I call it the CARE package. CARE stands for:

Clear

Analogies

Relevant

Examples

You are going to package your piece of writing in clear analogies or relevant examples—or both.

Think about some analogies from daily life that you can use to explain your concept with clarity. Then find some relatable stories you can tell to illustrate your points with impact.

Here's an analogy I used in one of my LinkedIn posts.

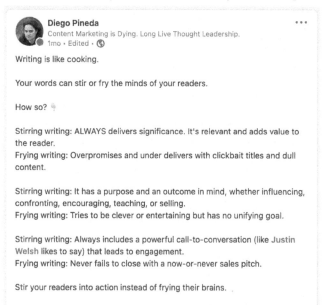

In his book, *The Art of Explanation*, Lee LeFever says: "Explanation is not focused on facts, laws, or specifics. Explanation is the art of showing why the facts, laws, and specifics make sense. By clarifying the reason an idea makes sense, we can put the facts into perspective. As such, explanation is the practice of packaging facts into a form that makes them easier to understand and apply." [4]

A solo thought leader goes beyond facts and figures and distills the why of things. A solo thought leader transcends theory and teaches how to apply knowledge. Aim for that in your blog posts.

3. Emotion-infused writing

In a digital world of influencers with glamorous lives, people are attracted to raw honesty and authenticity. Being vulnerable may feel risky, but it actually pays off in two ways:

- You don't have to pretend to be ultra successful all the time and show a fake person in your writing.
- Your readers can always tell when you are faking and actually respond better to weaknesses. When you share your story and life lessons, people respond.

You know you are writing with emotion when your readers save, share, and comment on your writing. If you are generating strong reactions and starting conversations, you know you are on the right path.

You want to write with emotion to create emotion. It has to be intentional. So, start with the goal in mind.

Do you want to convey excitement or anger? Sadness or hope? Get into that state before you start typing. Feel that emotion wash over you and then search in your mind for the words that best describe those emotions.

4. Use a formula to express your ideas

In my experience, you only need 3 things to communicate an idea:

- **A clear concept:** the brilliant business idea or step in your process.
- **A proof:** the research, stats, or business results that support your concept.
- **An example:** a story that illustrates your idea in action (this is the part readers will remember).

That's the formula I use to write my books and articles and even to outline my speeches. And it works.

It's similar to the formula used by Eddie Yoon to get published in *Harvard Business Review*:

- Have a provocative point of view that overturns conventional wisdom.
- Back it up with robust data or compelling case studies.
- Draw broadly applicable insights and implications that are useful for as wide an audience as possible across multiple industries.

What about podcasts?

Let's say the written word is not your strength, but speaking is. Then podcasts are a great option, as 37% of Americans (age 12+) listen to at least one podcast each month. [5]

One of the winning traits of a podcast is that listeners develop a level of intimacy with the host that is harder to achieve through writing. This is what my friend, Bernie Borges does. He is a seasoned (and awesome) marketer and a long-time podcast listener and podcast host himself.

"I've always appreciated that when you're listening to a podcast regularly," Bernie says, "you develop a connection with the host. And I've had people say that to me, although I never really opened up on the *Modern Marketing Engine* podcast. And I thought, wow, if that happened on a podcast where I never really opened up, you know, and I know how much I enjoy a connection to people who do open up, then that's something that I need to take that step forward and open up and talk about a topic that I have passion about." [6]

Just as we talked about infusing emotion into your writing and being true and honest in your blog posts, podcasting will allow you to do this at a deeper level. Your spoken words carry all the emotion and passion that sometimes is hard to put into words. When someone reads your prose, they are listening to your words in their own voice in their heads. But in a podcast, it's both your words and your voice.

Whether you podcast solo, in a monolog, or you use an interview format, you can come across as personal and real, and you will make a real connection with your audience.

"An interview based podcast is really good because you have two ways of connecting with people," says David Shriner-Cahn, the host of two podcasts for consultants, Going Solo and Smashing the Plateau. "You're connecting with the guests on your shows and you're connecting with the audience. And you're connecting around ideas. And if you like asking questions, it's a really good medium for doing that. Podcasts have helped me connect with guests, and build my reputation with them." [7]

How to Start a Podcast

1. Get the right equipment.
A podcast with crappy sound is a non-starter. You don't have to get a $300 or $400 microphone, but you should at least get a $50 or $60 microphone so you sound good.

2. Prepare for the long game.
The average podcast runs for 12 episodes before the podcaster gives up and stops.

"Go into it with the mindset that it's a marathon, not a sprint," Bernie says. "Go into it with the commitment to do this for not less than a year. And don't even expect to see a lot of results for less than a year."

You may see some results after a few months, but real traction won't start until you have built an audience. In fact, many potential guests won't consider coming to your podcast if you don't have at least 25 episodes out there.

3. Be consistent.
"I believe there are three elements that are important: consistency, frequency, and quality," says David Shriner-Cahn. "And the most important is consistency. We've produced podcast episodes every week since we launched in July of 2014, without fail. Now, they haven't always been an original episode recorded that week. I would say we have re-released a few but probably, like, 95% are actually original episodes."

Consistency depends on having a process and a system to plan, record, and publish your podcast. David, for instance, records in batches. Record several interviews or episodes in the same week, so you have a lead time of weeks.

Another technique is to release your podcast by seasons. In that case you can record a whole season in advance and then release it. This of course is not feasible if you are dealing with current news and issues. But for most thought leadership podcasts, a seasonal approach works.

How many episodes you should have in a season depends on the frequency (daily, weekly, monthly).

"Weekly is a good way to go," says Bernie, "because out of mind is out of sight. If you just do one a month, it's usually not going to be enough. Now if you're already famous and what I mean by that is an entrepreneur established within a certain niche, maybe monthly can work for them because people already know them."

4. Plan each episode.
The quality of the podcast will be a direct reflection of your preparation for it.

"Don't show up in front of the mic without knowing what you're going to cover," says Bernie. "If you're doing an interview-based podcast, prepare your guests, at least in advance. Provide the questions of the topic you're going to discuss and encourage them to have a microphone as well, so that they sound good."

5. Polish your episodes.
Whether you outsource or do it yourself, cleaning up and polishing your recordings is key.

"So you want to have a nice little intro and ideally a little music and then an outro," Bernie says. "It must be polished because you're competing against other podcasters, and when someone turns on a podcast for the first time they are going to make a quick judgment: What is the quality of the recording and the quality of the content? Does it appeal to me? Do I want to stay here and listen to this? I've turned on podcasts where I just bailed because I didn't like the quality of the production, I didn't feel they were professional."

6. Market your podcast.
Once you have the audio recording ready and publish it, you have to get the word out. Bernie recommends writing a blog post for each episode, an article summarizing the podcast so you get some SEO value and where people can decide if they want to listen to the whole episode.

There are many platforms you can use to distribute your podcast, the most popular being Spotify and Apple Podcasts. Get on as many platforms as you can and promote the heck out of your podcast in social media (which we are going to talk about next).

Dominate Social Media

Justin Welsh was an executive at a SaaS company when he decided he had enough of working for others and it was time to go on his own. He had built his expertise in building sales teams over the years and had a lot to teach others. He knew he could have a thriving consulting business.

"I had a hypothesis," he says. "And it was that if I wanted to go out on my own, getting some attention would be really important. And I know as a sales and marketing person that the more people are reading what you write, seeing your face, seeing your name, the more familiar they become with you as a person and the way that you think, the more likely they are to buy something from you down the road, if you serve their needs."

The way forward for Justin was to use social media.

"Social media is the vehicle that takes your thoughts and delivers them to the masses. But in order to get traction, you have to know what you're talking about. And I think that's something that people overlook a lot. You need to talk about things that you fully understand. There are always people that are behind you in their journey, who don't yet understand those things. So your goal using social media is to show people your expertise and you can do that through solving their problems, sharing best practices, walking them step-by-step through ways to do something better, challenging the way that they're thinking, showing them the behind-the-scenes."

Justin started posting content around sales and his experience building a large sales organization up to 50 million in recurring revenue. After a while, most of the questions he received were not about sales but about how he was using social media.

"I didn't consider myself an expert at that at all," he says, "but then I looked around and recognized I had a hundred and some thousand followers on one platform. I was making money, I was building businesses. So I thought to myself, okay, there's something here. I know something about this and there's a lot of people who are much earlier than me on the journey. I'm not going to go out and try and teach Gary Vaynerchuk how to use social media. He doesn't need my help. He's way further ahead than I am. So, what I'm trying to do is to work with people who are on the beginning part of the journey, help them get their traction. And so now I write content about that and I share that through social media."

In June of 2018, Justin wrote his first ever piece of content on LinkedIn, but it got no traction. He didn't write again until October of 2018. Even then he was sporadic and got absolutely nowhere. But in 2019, he made a commitment to write every single weekday on LinkedIn with the goal of making a name for himself on the internet. It took 5 months, but he finally wrote a post that was seen more than 1.24 million times. Interestingly, that post was his origin story.

A couple of years later, Justin dominated LinkedIn with more than 140,000 followers, a popular online course, and a thriving membership community. He is now rapidly growing his following on Twitter as well.

The first step in dominating social media is to start by focusing on one platform.

Where does your niche hang out? Which is their favorite social network?

You may have a good sense of where they are because of your conversations with them. Or you may have not conducted any research yet and believe that they may be in your own favorite social media platform.

Just in case, double-check what you think with this data compiled by Hootsuite. [8]

Facebook
- 21.4% of all Facebook users are ages 45 and older. (But seniors are the fastest-growing Facebook age demographic.)
- 32.4% of all Facebook users are ages 25 to 34.
- More males (56.4%) than females (43.6%) use Facebook; Male users ages 25 to 34 make up the biggest demographic of Facebook users.

Instagram

- 51% of all Instagram users worldwide are female.
- One third of Instagram's users are ages 25 to 34.
- Instagram is also popular among younger users. Instagram is the most-used social media platform among American teenagers.

LinkedIn

- 43% of users are female; 57% are male.
- 59.9% of all LinkedIn users worldwide are age 25 to 34. The next biggest user base of this social platform is the 18 to 24 age group, making up 20.3%.
- This age distribution differs in the U.S: 40% of American internet users ages 46-55 had used the platform.

Twitter

- 28.9% of Twitter users worldwide are between the ages of 24 and 34. 57.1% of Twitter users worldwide are ages 25 to 49.
- Twitter is used more by males than females. 70% of Twitter's advertising audience are male and 30% are female.

YouTube

- As of September 2020, 72% of all male internet users in the U.S. used YouTube. That number is the same for females: 72% of American females who use the internet will use YouTube.
- 77% of internet users in the U.S. ages 15 to 25 use YouTube.

For Justin, it was LinkedIn, where most B2B and SaaS leaders hang out.

For Diana Pineda, it was Facebook, where she could reach Gen Xers, the parents of her students. Now she is experimenting with TikTok to appeal directly to Gen Z.

Jaime Jay does live streaming, going out on Facebook, LinkedIn Live, and YouTube, to reach small business owners.

Whichever platform you choose, you must commit to post everyday about one or two topics for which you want to be known. Many newcomers make the mistake of posting about whatever comes to mind and make it hard for people to decide if they should follow them or not.

Here's what most people do on social media:

- Scroll down the feed without engaging.
- Write random posts about whatever comes to mind.
- Take, take, take.
- Worry about the future.
- Follow trends.

But here's what solo educators do:

- Engage in conversations with their network.
- Post strategically about their niche.
- Give, give, give.
- Create their future.
- Set trends.

As you create content in social media, consider how you want your audience to respond and encourage conversations around your topics with questions and calls to conversations.

Don't be boring, be relevant, come up with new content, don't become predictable.

Give value and generate engagement. How do you provide value? By writing in three tenses:

- **Past:** reflect on past experiences to teach life lessons.
- **Present:** describe your current wins and failures to encourage others on a similar journey.
- **Future:** provide professional insights into what's coming for your industry.

Your goal is to create a community of followers, but you won't achieve that only by posting and expecting people to find you. You must engage with other creators and provide insightful comments on their posts. I've done this with incredible results. Just by commenting on Justin's LinkedIn posts, for example, I get exposure to thousands of people, some who then become my followers.

As a journalism major with a minor in philosophy, I always stood out with my philosophy papers. Philosophy professors said my essays were surprisingly clear, like a good newspaper article. They were used to the dense and cryptic writing of my classmates, so my assignments were a breath of fresh air.

If that's true for academics, it must be true for your readers as well. Great thought leadership writing must have the 4 S's:

- **Short:** Avoid fluff and repetition. Your writing should solve a problem, not impress the reader with how much you know.
- **Simple:** Leave complexity to philosophy students. Your writing should bring clarity, not confusion.

- **Straight:** Say what you mean in conversational language, direct and to the point.
- **Specific:** It's about what the reader cares for. Write with your audience in mind.

If you want your writing to be effective, ditch Aristotelian language and embrace your inner journalist. Your readers will thank you.

Social Media is a Long-Term Strategy

Publishing educational content online won't yield thousands of followers immediately.

It may take a while to gain traction and momentum but it requires you to be consistently delivering value, even if it's for an audience of a few people. All the solo thought leaders with massive impact started one day with zero followers.

Instant gratification is a common thing these days, and you'll probably get pitches for joining LinkedIn pods (groups of people who will like and comment on each other's posts) or buy Instagram followers (mostly thousands of fake accounts).

None of these hacks will help you become a solo thought leader.

"The algorithm is messing up my views!" is something I hear a lot on LinkedIn.

But do you know what the real problem is? Lousy writing.

People are trying all sorts of gimmicks to trick the algorithm and get their views up, but their writing still sucks. Ergo, their engagement sucks.

My advice: focus on improving your writing and eventually your views and your sales will go up.

Take a copywriting class, read a book. Write and rewrite.

Ask for feedback and learn from writers you admire. It may not give you a quick spike in views, but once it does, you'll know you have true followers and fans and not just accidental readers brought by tricking the algorithm.

Viveka von Rosen says that the most important thing is to actually know what you're talking about.

"Just get the information out there, whether you blog, whether you're writing books, whether you're posting updates, whatever that looks like," she says. "Be consistent with it, be thoughtful, and make it quality content. I get that there's a lot of people on TikTok or Instagram who are insta-famous because they're cute and they do a little dance. Good for them, but I don't know how sustainable that is. But for people in business who want to create credibility and thought leadership, you really have to know what you're talking about and it takes time. There's not a lot of overnight sensations who actually have sticking power. So just be patient and know that five to six years down the road, someone will recognize you as an overnight success, which happened to me. That was really funny. I was written up in some article as the overnight LinkedIn expert, the overnight success. And I'm like, 'Dude, I've been at this for six years already. Are you kidding me right now?' But okay. I'll take it."

Become a Public Speaker

The oldest form of education is speaking in front of an audience. Depending on your industry, being a popular keynote speaker will be crucial to establishing your authority (or not). Either way, public speaking is part of expanding your message and educating your audience.

"Some people would rather die than be on stage," says Viveka, "but if you can get comfortable with being onstage and being a speaker, that can help to differentiate you and position yourself as a thought leader."

If you are uncomfortable being on stage or in front of a camera, Viveka recommends that you join a Toastmasters group.

"Almost everyone that I talk to of my speaker friends who were terrified of the stage joined Toastmasters and that made all the difference for them."

As you get started, jump at any opportunity to speak, either live or online, in front of an audience. Viveka regrets turning down an opportunity to speak at TEDx years ago.

"I'm an idiot. I turned down TEDx because it wasn't TED. I thought the only TED worth doing was TED, so when they started coming out with TEDx, I was asked not once but twice to do a TEDx talk and I turned them both down because I was like, that's too much work and it's no big deal. That's a lost opportunity there. But if you can get the opportunity to do a TEDx, it will really make a difference in your own speaking. Plus, it looks really good on your LinkedIn banner."

David Meerman Scott has positioned himself as a virtual keynote speaker in the Covid era. He has decades of experience delivering marketing and business growth presentations in over 40 countries, focusing on providing practical advice and entertainment. "I customize my virtual or in-person keynotes and masterclasses for each audience," he writes on his website. "My goal is to make your event amazing. The core of every event I speak at is motivating your audience to take action and succeed."

For instance, David promotes audience interaction at virtual talks by using polling, chats, breakout rooms, and social media.

The key is not to be just one more public speaker with the same formula. Offering customized, entertaining events is a great way to stand out.

Create Digital Products and Training Programs

The most popular online courses are about creating and selling online courses. And if you want to learn anything, just go to YouTube, where people watch educational content 500 million times a day, according to Internal YouTube Data (from 2017, so imagine now!).

Udemy is a marketplace where people pay $10 to $20 on average to learn coding, selling techniques, or digital marketing. And if you want something more sophisticated, navigate over to Udacity for a nanodegree in Data Science, Artificial Intelligence, Product Management, and more.

Since 2012, the web has been inundated with MOOCs (massively open online courses) with on-demand videos and learning materials available for free and for a nominal fee. Some of them by the best professors in the world.

Want a class from an Ivy League prof? Go to Coursera. Want a class with a best-selling author or musician or a famous chef? Sign up for Masterclass.

We all have signed up for them, but very few complete them. Completion rates for these courses are 3 to 6 percent. [9]

So why create another online course?

You're right, don't create just another online course. Create something different like only a solo thought leader could.

A popular upgrade to MOOCs are Cohort-Based Courses (CBCs). These are also online courses but the group advances together with a community and interactive learning. CBCs have a live component and a start and finish dates, so there is accountability and deadlines, which result in higher completion rates. Instead of passively consuming content like in a MOOC, students practice active learning and interact with an instructor.

If you are doing a CBC, you can charge premium prices (between $500 and $5,000), because they are more than videos. They can include:

- Live classes
- 1:1 coaching
- Personalized curriculum
- Community features
- Group calls
- Feedback on assignments
- Office hours for answering questions
- Insider information
- Mastermind features
- Access to exclusive tech tools

Bob Goodwin, for example, created a course for job seekers called *Making your Own Weather*, around attitude, personal branding, outreach interviewing, and negotiating. The content of the course is no different from other courses in the market. But Bob added a second element that makes his offer stand out.

"I noticed that there was no enabling technology for people searching for a job," Bob says. "People literally run their job search off sticky notes, the back of their Capital One bill, or a Google sheet or Excel. Basically what they're doing is building their own CRM tool. They are adding information like, who did I talk to, what did we talk about, who introduced us, which resume did I send them, what am I supposed to do next. Well, that's what CRM does. It helps you manage your portfolio of opportunities and all your contacts, your activities and your calendar. So, I repurposed a CRM tool to mirror what I think a proper sales funnel should look like and then all the data elements people are trying to keep up with in their spreadsheets and their Google Gmail and all this stuff."

Bob's CRM tool is integrated with Crunchbase, a database of 1.5 million companies, that tells you which companies are getting funding and, hence, hiring. This is what a typical salesperson would do to build a list of prospects, but now Bob provides those tools to job seekers.

So, how can you create innovative digital products and courses to educate your audience?

Perhaps instead of just teaching skills, train and certify others to replicate your framework or methodology. Create a comprehensive curriculum, a training institute, a certification program, or even franchises of your thought leadership ideas.

Build a Community

An online community can be a great add-on to your online course, or it can be a stand-alone offer.

For instance, after taking Justin Welsh's course, I joined his *Audience & Income* online community, where I met some amazing solopreneurs who are growing their business online. Justin promotes the A&I Community inside his courses and on his website.

David Shriner-Cahn, on the other hand, runs the *Smashing the Plateau Private Community*, for consultants to meet and support one another, get answers to burning questions, learn from experts, participate in growth challenges, and more.

"I've always been involved in communities," he says, "and then I realized that my audience deals with isolation. Here are these folks who come out of this sort of corporate cocoon and they're like thrown to the wind and they really struggle. What they need is a community of like-minded people where it's a safe place, a caring place where they can let their hair down a little bit, talk about where they're challenged, get some help and you know, I'm good at community building and I figured I should probably put two and two together and start my own community."

You don't need fancy software or expensive tech to run a community. Justin runs his community with Slack, which has a free version. Other free tools for community building are Discord and Facebook Groups.

Marcus Chan has a private Facebook Group of almost three thousand members, where he posts sales training videos (both live and recorded), and answers member's questions. Because people can join for free and get a taste for Marcus' expertise, the Facebook Group also serves as a lead generation channel, where many members end up buying his courses.

David Shriner-Cahn says that to run a vibrant community you must be an active listener. "You got to listen to what people are talking about, what they need and just be in there and be a good servant. Just serve them. As a community leader, the more you make it about them and not about you, the better the community will be. Running a community effectively is not for people with big egos."

Checklist

☑ I have crafted my own origin story and I'm sharing it through different channels.

☑ I have a personal website with a custom domain.

☑ I have a blog or podcast where I publish content relevant to my audience weekly.

☑ I have picked one or two social media networks where my audience hangs out and I'm posting thought leadership content every weekday.

☑ I have a public speaking track (list of topics) and I'm looking for opportunities to speak in front of others.

☑ I have a digital product or training program that I use to educate my followers and grow my business.

☑ I have created a community of followers (free or paid) where my niche audience can share ideas and I can provide value for them.

STEP 5
THE SOLO STAR

Gather social proof and media attention

Chapter 7

"It's great to be called a thought leader by the industry and your peers. Just don't put it in your own bio."

That's the subtitle of an Inc. magazine article by Sangram Vajre, Chief Evangelist and Co-Founder at Terminus. [1]

Sangram has everything a thought leader should have: a popular business podcast, a newsletter with more than 27,000 subscribers, over 10 million views, a private mastermind group for marketing leaders, and three published books (one of them a Wall Street Journal and USA Today best-seller). Plus, he is a sought-after keynote speaker.

Still, he doesn't like to call himself a thought leader. He argues that the title of "thought leader" is an honor to be earned and using it on your bio sounds egotistical.

"Telling someone you're a thought leader is like telling people you're rich," Sangram writes. "It usually means you aren't, and it's incredibly gauche. Real thought leaders don't have to tell people; their actions give them away. It's a nice thing for someone else to call you, but an obnoxious thing to call yourself."

In a world of celebrities and inflated egos, Sangram's advice seems naive, but it's true. As a solopreneur your actions have to speak for themselves. Thought leadership is not about just being the expert and knowing the theory, but being in the trenches, creating changes and having an impact in the real world. It's about practicing what you preach and taking massive action so people will follow your example.

Humility goes a long way when you start gaining recognition for your ideas, so:

- Be approachable and friendly (don't be a snob!).
- Treat everyone with dignity.
- Respond to messages and connect with people.
- Help others become thought leaders.

When you do this, your clout will increase and others will start singing your praises. But don't let it go to your head.

The Solo Mindset: "It's Not About Me!"

As a solopreneur, you may feel it's you against the world, or that you have to prove your critics wrong. And sometimes that is a good motivator. But the fact that you run a business of one doesn't mean the business is about you.

The solo thought leader embraces a selfless mindset because the definition of leadership itself implies inspiring others and working with a team toward certain goals.

In that sense, your content or messaging should not be about you but about helping your audience.

And here lies one of the fundamental differences between an influencer and a thought leader.

Brittany Hennessy, author of Influencer, defines "influencer" as someone who has "social currency," meaning that when she speaks, her audience listens, acts, and buys. [2]

Many influencers create a cult following around their lavish lifestyle (whether fake or real) or their physique. A few of them will feature their art or craft and some sort of expertise (in beauty, health, or fitness, for example) but usually they are the centerpiece of their posts. Some consider them just people a few notches below the celebrity status but with enough clout to attract sponsors and fans.

According to Hennessy, if you were an influencer you would spend "days and nights creating content for audiences so fickle they can, and will, stop following you because you posted your Tuesday video on Wednesday. Or because they didn't like the color of your manicure in that ice cream photo. Or because—and I have seen this—you changed your eyebrows, you now look like "a weird bird," and your face makes them uncomfortable."

The solo mindset, on the other hand, is about deeply understanding its audience. And I learned some great lessons about this from the popular comedic series Ted Lasso.

In case you haven't met Ted, he's an American football coach from Kansas who ends up coaching a football (soccer) team in England, despite knowing nothing about the game. That, of course, lends itself for some quirky humor.

Ted is as American as you can get, referencing American pop culture and using slang in every other sentence, to the dismay of his British listeners.

"Now don't you fret, Boba Fett."

"Think of me as his own personal Mr. Miyagi. Except without all that extra yard work."

"What's the word, Larry Bird,"

"Yes sir, Steve Kerr".

"You beating yourself up is like Woody Allen playing the clarinet. I don't want to hear it."

Worst yet, he doesn't seem to try too hard to understand the language of his audience. He avoids talking about football and when his players mention some game specifics, he says something like this: "One more person says something to me and Beard don't understand, I'm gonna have one of my son's classic temper tantrums. It's basically just him calling me a bunch of silly names, you know, like, I don't know, "dummy head" or "poo-poo face" "pee-pee fingers."

That's great for comedy, but not for thought leadership. Communicating like a solo thought leader requires you to speak the language of your audience. I call it the Audience Mind Frame: Putting yourself in your reader's mind (not shoes).

Ask yourself:

- What is my audience's level of understanding and previous knowledge about this topic?
- Is there something obvious to me that might not be obvious to them?
- What is their cultural and social background?
- How do they see the world and how does it differ from my worldview?

Just the other day I was talking with Bob Goodwin, who spent many years talking to salespeople but recently went solo to help people who want to make a career change.

"You have to learn people's language," Bob said. "Actually, my LinkedIn post this morning said, the very first line in it, I'm stuck. Because that's what people say: I'm stuck. So I'm going to use your words right back to you in a way that you'll understand. I did 30 one-on-one interviews last year with people that I had helped previously, and very specifically what I was looking for was the emotions that they were feeling and the words that they used. I even built a word cloud. Why? To be able to understand what's the language that my customers are using so that I can speak to them, not in my weird way or even overly fancy way, but in a way that they can say, 'Yep, that is me, you get me.'"

Even if you want to persuade or challenge the beliefs of your audience, you must understand where they are coming from. Meet them where they are before taking them where they should be.

I realized how tricky this can be when I started writing children's fiction. My target readers were middle grade kids, so every word choice had to be at their level. Not only that, but I was writing in first person from the point of view of my main characters: a 12-year-old boy and his 10-year-old sister. So, when writing a scene, I had to think, how would a 10-year-old girl would feel, act, and express herself in this particular situation?

I'm a guy in my 40s, so I had to do some research. As I mentioned before, my wife runs an e-school and I got to teach creative writing to kids that age. I learned their slang, what kind of jokes made them laugh, their worries, and what they are curious about.

For example, moving to a new house is a big deal for them, so that is a topic they care about. Or school dynamics, or the expectations of their parents. It's very different from the topics I wrote about for my novels for an adult audience, which dealt with politics and life or death situations.

"Come on, Diego, I already know my audience deeply," you might say. "I'm an expert in my field."

Cool. Just make sure you are not affected by the curse of knowledge: assuming your audience understands what you are saying just because you do.

Does that mean you should not do self-promotion?

Very few people love self-promotion. They either hate it or see it as a necessary evil.

I did one of the infamous LinkedIn polls asking people what they thought about self-promotion. Here are the results.

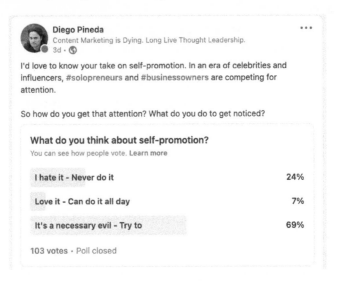

The discussion in the comments got interesting. One person said: "The issue is why are you doing what you're doing. Self promotion for the sake of self promotion makes you Gary VeeD, Grant Cardone and all the other me disease assholes." (sic)

Another one said: "Instead of promoting yourself, promote the ways you help people—and it won't feel like a 'necessary evil' or self-promotion. If your product or service is rock-solid, marketing it becomes the most ethical thing you can do. And if it's not rock-solid—go back to the drawing board."

And a third one said: "Promoting yourself is a subset of establishing a personal brand. If all one does is self promotion—it doesn't attract clients. Clients don't care about how amazing we think we are. They care about what value you can add, what your own values are and how you can help them. Through personal branding they get to know who we are and that is what attracts them to us."

The consensus is that you should promote your value, what you do to help others, not yourself. I agree.

Justin Welsh says you must give 80% of the time and only ask 20% of the time. For example, if you post five times a week on social media, let four posts be about giving value, advice, and thought leadership, and one post about asking people to buy your products.

Gather Social Proof

I don't know about you, but the first thing I do when browsing a book or some product on Amazon is head down to the reviews. It's like an instinct to seek confirmation from the tribe before trusting someone else and purchasing a product.

And it's the same with solo thought leaders, whether you are selling something or not (but you better be).

There are many ways to gather social proof, including good ol' fashioned testimonials, LinkedIn recommendations, and media mentions. Let's see how you can leverage them.

Testimonials

One thing that caught my attention when I first visited Justin Welsh's sales page was the amount of testimonials he has (both video and text). It was then an easy decision to buy his course.

He says testimonials do a few things:

- They let you know that people find your products and services valuable. If people aren't leaving reviews or testimonials, then it's likely your products aren't having a major impact on them.
- They improve conversions on your website. Featuring testimonials gives prospects more confidence to buy your products. Place them near the purchase button to improve conversion.
- They increase word-of-mouth. The more people are impacted positively by your products, the more likely they are to talk to other people. This helps drive more sales through things like affiliate programs.

Bob Goodwin likes to call testimonials, "success stories." He has these success stories all over his website.

"I'm doing LinkedIn live now because it's my natural medium. And the first episode was a success story, basically a testimonial. Then I had a career coach the second week, so it was a little more topical. But last week it was a guy that I had helped who had a story of overcoming some obstacles in the interview process in a way that would really resonate with people. So, I use testimonials selectively, not all the time, in the LinkedIn Lives."

Marcus Chan says your followers only care about getting results.

"You have to make sure your stuff actually works," Marcus says. "When you do that, when you deliver transformation, you're going to get testimonials, you get proof, you get screenshots and get all these things. Every single day I get emails and messages from people in my program telling me of their success. 'I just closed this deal. I got promoted.' I got one yesterday from a sales rep. He is now number two out of 600 reps. It's insane, but it's because I continue to work to improve the products."

Ask your clients for feedback and why they would recommend your products. Then use the feedback to improve and the recommendation to promote your offerings.

LinkedIn Recommendations

Another form of social proof on LinkedIn is recommendations. Ask colleagues or clients to add a testimonial of your work and your character to your profile, highlighting the results and the contributions you made. One way to obtain recommendations is by giving them yourself, then asking others to return the favor.

Media Mentions and Quotes

It may sound old fashioned to talk to the media and try to get quoted by journalists, because there are so many more ways people consume media today that the chances that people will see your quote in a newspaper or TV show is not that high.

David Meerman Scott, who knows a lot about PR and publicity, says that it has become less important to get quoted in the media for the direct results of immediate exposure, but that the indirect results are super powerful.

"Here's the indirect reason," he says. "Getting quoted is important because you can put it on your website and you can share it on your social media. So if you get quoted in The Wall Street Journal, all of a sudden on your website and on your social media, you can say 'Hey, I was just quoted in The

Wall Street Journal,' and that gives you some credibility. So, I think that it's still important to get quoted in mainstream media. You then have sort of a stamp of approval that says, 'Oh, I know enough about what I do that I can get quoted in this particular publication or this particular television station.' It might be good."

Don't chase random publications, though. Think what publications would add credibility and authority in the eyes of your audience. Marcus Chan, who has been quoted by Forbes, MarketWatch, and Yahoo! Finance says salespeople don't care much about those.

However, when he was quoted by Salesforce or recognized as a *LinkedIn Top Voice*, it was a different story. People started reaching out to him and following his publications because of those mentions.

"What you want to think about is which publications resonate the most with your target market," Marcus says. "If there's an industry-specific podcast or magazine, or a smart solution in your industry, those are the ones you want to be able to get their attention."

So how do you obtain your social proof? Here are some ideas:

- Include a call-to-action in your digital products and courses for people to submit testimonials.
- Add a form on your site or a link to a Google survey, what they liked and disliked, and whether they would recommend you to others.
- Use tools like testimonial.io to get video testimonials.
- Immediately after a coaching call, email your client and ask them for a testimonial.

- Go to your LinkedIn Profile and click on "Ask for a recommendation" in the Recommendations section. Then select the person you want to ask and add a personal note, such as "Hey, Johnny, I hope you found my call/services helpful. If you think this would be helpful to others, would you please consider submitting a recommendation? Thanks!"
- For media quotes, send out press releases, develop relationships with journalists, or join HARO (helpareporter.com) as a source.

Many people stop at gathering social proof and posting it online. But you can go further and turn clients into referral sources.

You deliberately ask a happy client, "Do you know one person who would benefit from this experience?"

They don't want to look dumb and say they don't know anyone. They'll probably say they know more than one person, that they know two or three. But don't ask for more than one because you don't want them to feel pressured to come up with a list of names. Don't use the word referral either.

The best way to phrase the question is: "Do you know one person who would benefit from this experience?" Then they will go to their database and send you people to meet with. It's a win-win scenario.

Checklist

☑ I understand that my content and messaging is not about me, but about my customers.

☑ I am gathering testimonials and recommendations from my clients.

☑ I am reaching out to the media and establishing relationships with journalists and trade publications in my industry.

STEP 6
THE SOLO BUSINESS
OWNER

Create scalable systems and processes

Chapter 8

Thought leadership requires time to think.

Think about thinking, think about the future, think about new ideas and categories.

It also requires time to write down those ideas, develop frameworks and processes, and educate your audience through different channels. And on top of that, you still have to run your business as a solopreneur and make money to pay the bills.

This is the old conflict between the tyranny of the urgent and the priority of the important. In his brilliant book, *Making Money is Killing your Business*, Chuck Blakeman says:

"The Tyranny of the Urgent keeps us focused on making money. The Priority of the Important helps us build a business that makes money for us. Don't get me wrong, you have to make money. Okay, not you, the business. The problem is that the business teaches us to use our own personal time to make money. This is also called bootstrapping, pulling a business up by its own bootstraps. If we sell a widget, we take the profits to buy two more, sell those and buy four more. Unless you take big investment money up front, you're likely to be the one making the widgets in the early stages of your business. If you're growing into business by bootstrapping, you have to fight the habit of focusing on making money yourself. Being the principal producer in your business will almost certainly keep you from building a business that makes money while you're on vacation." [1]

So, if you want to be a solo thought leader, you must figure out how to be a real business owner—that is, you set up systems and processes so that you decide how the business is going to run for you instead of you running for your business.

Chuck developed a concept called business maturity, which means that a business is mature when the owner can go on vacation for 4 weeks or more (and not work during that time) and when she comes back, the business is still making money and running at full speed.

This was Jaime Jay's case, although he was not on vacation.

On March 1st of 2020, Jaime's mother passed away. But in January and February, Jaime had to split his time between his company in Springfield, Missouri, and California, where his mother had been.

"I spent the first seven weeks with my mom with a one-week break coming back here," he says. "I got a call from the doctor that I had to go back. Well, I didn't work at all for those two months. Maybe a couple phone calls. That was it. And I came back to a company with more clients than when I left and that speaks volumes to systems and processes and having the team members in the right role doing the correct responsibilities."

What is your Business Model?

What do you want out of your business? How much money do you want to make and for what purpose? The answer to those questions will determine your business model.

"As a solopreneur," says David Shriner-Cahn, "I can have the business model where I want to spend my time fixing certain kinds of problems and I only need three to five clients that pay me three to five thousand dollars a month each, and they have a consistent need for what I offer, so I don't have a lot of turnover. That's actually a good business model for me and how I want to live my life."

This model is common for coaches and consultants who offer 1:1 consultations at a high price, or consult with companies for a monthly retainer. This model can give you a good life-style and income, but it's not scalable and will always depend on you trading time for money.

"Other people may say," David says, "Well, I'd like to build a business where I'm solving the same kinds of problems, but I want the business to be able to grow in net income while at the same time I'm putting less and less of my time into the business. There's no need for me to work X number of hours per week consistently. I'm working less and less over time and it produces more and more money for me."

David calls this model *FIRE: Financial Independence, Retire Early.* "This is the model where I can build something that creates enough of what I need for my personal finances that I don't have to work in it. So, you got to figure out what business model is most important to you. Once you figure that out, then you can put all the pieces together."

This is the model that makes more sense for solo thought leaders, in my opinion. Let me show you why.

The Solo Business Owner's Game

Circa 2012, I was a business consultant with the Crankset Group in Vancouver. One of my clients, George, ran a landscaping business. He wanted me to help him get more clients. But I had a hunch that that was not what he needed.

"Let's say I help you get more clients," I said. "Can you serve them?"

He thought for a while and said, "No, I don't have time."

"How many hours are you working every week?"

"About 80 hours."

I opened the calculator on my phone. "And how much money are you taking home every month?"

"$1,800."

I divided that 1,800 by the 240 hours he worked per month. Then I showed him the result.

"You are making $7.50 an hour. You could make more working at McDonald's and you could have the weekends off. You don't need more clients, you need to organize yourself and start delegating."

Turns out he was doing everything in his business, from manual labor to invoicing and sales, plus fixing the mistakes his untrained employees made every day. So, we worked on a plan to free his time.

The solo business owner's game is this: How do I make more money in less time?

Have you tried to make more money in more time? That's pretty easy, right? Until you run out of time. You only have 168 hours in a week. So, you can only make so much money doing that.

Now, it's also easy to make less money in less time. If you just want to go live under a bridge or you stop working, you'll make less money in less time. That's not a good game to play either. The game that a business owner should play is how to make more money in less time. If you are not playing that game, do not call yourself a business owner yet. Call yourself a proprietor or a craftsman or a tradesman or anything you want, but don't you dare call yourself a business owner until you decide to play the game of making more money in less time. Because that's how business owners think.

This is what I told George:

You are going to make a list or a map of every activity in your business, from getting a client to closing a deal and delivering the product and you are going to identify which ones you are doing.

Then for each task, you are going to ask, is this the best and highest use of my time? If the answer is no, then ask yourself, how do I do this for the last time?

There are three ways of doing something for the last time:

- **Delegation:** get somebody else to do it, like invoicing or accounting.
- **Automation:** set up a system (a software, or app) to take care of it, like email autoresponders.
- **Elimination:** perhaps that task is no longer necessary, so just get rid of it.

Sounds like common sense. So, why don't solopreneurs do this more often? Because they think that by doing simple things like answering emails or scheduling meetings, they are saving money. "Why am I sending out invoices? I'm saving $15 an hour." That's not a solo business owner's mindset.

The math has to change. Let's say that you're worth $200/hour, that's how much you want to make. So, when you spend time sending invoices, you're not saving $15, you're losing $185 an hour.

You could be out there consulting, coaching someone, closing a big deal, and make $200 an hour, while paying

$150 for ten hours of a distant assistant, for example, to do the invoicing. Even then, you would turn out a profit of $50, working less time.

The Delegation Roadmap

Jaime Jay's top advice for solopreneurs is to prepare to hire somebody right now, even if you don't need somebody or you can't afford it. And the way you prepare is by starting the documentation process.

"Anything that you do, do it as if it's the last time you're ever going to do it," he says. "Document, document, document. Whether you're checking your email, scheduling a call, meeting a client, whatever it is. What do you do to prepare to meet that client? What do you do to schedule an appointment? Do you have calendar software? What kind of email are you using? How do you check your emails? How do you categorize your emails? Start documenting everything with a delegation roadmap."

A delegation roadmap is where you list everything out that you do on a given day, any repeatable tasks, and then assign two values to each task:

1. Is it something that I can delegate or is this something that I must do?

2. Does this particular task give me energy or drains me?

Managing email, for example, is something that doesn't give most people energy. So, you could delegate that task. While a podcast interview, for instance, is something you must do as a subject matter expert. And if you are serious about thought leadership, then it should be something that energizes you and that you enjoy.

"Once you have a list of the things that you can delegate and that do not give you energy," Jaime says, "take the top three that are the biggest thorns in your side, the biggest pains, and make a subset list. Then take number one and document that. For example, create a video walk-through on how you check your email."

With that documentation, you can later hire anyone to do those tasks and they won't have to worry about pulling stuff out of your head.

"If you ever decide to exit a business and you don't have systems and processes documented, then you really have to worry about the valuation of that business. Because without the solopreneur there, the company doesn't exist. The goal is that down the road you can be replaceable."

Create a Strategic Plan

I recently saw a LinkedIn post that caught my attention. It was from Bill Sherman, a thought leadership consultant for B2B clients. He said:

"If thought leadership = ideas + strategy + execution—
What's the term that most people overlook?
I've worked with many individuals and organizations.
And I've seen a very common misstep.
People try to replace strategy with tactics.
And that works for a little while.
They make themselves incredibly busy—
Creating assets. Speaking. Webinars. Writing.
It feels so good to be busy.
To put ideas out into the world.

But without a strategy, ideas rarely reach scale.
The ideas get lost in the noise.
And they create little impact.
Strategy is essential to thought leadership.
But it requires you to stop being busy.
And think about *why* you're putting ideas out into the world.
How does your thought leadership work connect to your business objectives?
How will you know if your ideas are creating impact?
Where should you invest your resources (time, energy, money)?"

This is spot on. Just as you would have a strategic plan for your business, you should have a strategic plan for becoming a solo thought leader. And I would argue that it is the same plan.

Traditional business planning has taught us that the most important part of planning is to plan the "middle" of the process—the "how," in great detail, then follow that plan at all costs. You don't need to do that. Use what Chuck Blakeman calls the 2.1 Plan, which has three simple questions:

1) Where am I?
2) Where do I want to end up?
2.1) What are the next few steps?

Why 2.1 and not 3? Because to be a 3, the question would be: How do I get all the way from #1 to #2?

Which is not feasible to answer because there are too many variables in business to accurately plan all the way from where you are to where you want to end up. Unless you have a fully functional and accurate crystal ball. Do you happen to have one? No? I thought so.

We can only get started and figure out the next steps as we go.

And the way to do that is ditching the idea of a 5-year business plan and work on a simple, two-page strategic plan that will show you the next steps.

This is the same strategic plan I taught my clients when I was with the Crankset Group and that I've used to run all my businesses. Here, I've adapted it a bit to match the solo thought leader framework.

The plan has four basic parts: Vision, Mission, Strategies, and Goals.

Vision

The vision answers the question "Why?" and it's directly related to your point of view as a thought leader. This is your ultimate goal, the unique vision you stand for.

Examples:

- Create wealth and abundance for myself and others. (Financial advisor)
- Champion freedom through digital entrepreneurship. (Business consultant)
- Live and teach others to live a creative and passionate life doing what we love. (Life coach)

Mission

The mission answers the question "What?" and focuses on the results you want for your business and career. Examples:

- Help business owners make more money in less time and get back to the passion that brought them into business, so they can build a mature business in support of their lifetime goals. (Chuck Blakeman's mission)

• Help aspiring authors put their great ideas into writing and release their books into the world. (My mission as a book coach)

• Help solopreneurs discover their unique abilities (a.k.a. superpowers) and put them into the service of others. (John Arms)

Strategies

The strategies tell you "how" you are going to accomplish your mission. You can write down strategies that you think will work in the next one or two years, and update them as time goes by (as your business and influence grows, you will need new strategies).

Some strategies examples include:

- Live workshops and seminars for business owners
- Books and other publications
- Online courses
- 1:1 Coaching
- Virtual communities

Goals

The goals answer the questions "What and when?" and are divided into annual (12 months), quarterly (3 months), and monthly goals. They should be, of course, SMART goals.

For the annual goals, write down your big projects for the coming year (write a book series, launch a cohort course, delegate all the admin tasks of your business, etc.) and the date you will complete them. These are usually things that will take 7 or more months to complete.

Each annual goal must be tied to one or more strategies in the plan, because the goals exist to carry out your strategies, and your strategies exist to fulfill your mission.

The quarterly goals answer the question, "What do I have to do this quarter to complete my annual goals?" and the monthly objectives or actions answer, "What do I have to do this month to complete the quarterly goals?" Every quarterly goal must be tied to an annual goal and every monthly action should be tied to a quarterly goal.

To see what the plan looks like when completed and to download a free template you can use, go to *solothoughtleader.com/plan.*

Use the Strategic Plan to make decisions every week and month in your business. This is a dynamic, living, changing document that evolves as your business grows.

WEEKLY: Once a week, block out 15-30 minutes to review your Monthly Action Plans with this question in mind: What do I have to do this week to make sure this Monthly Action Plan is achieved? Then block out whatever time you need that week to get it done.

MONTHLY: Once a month, extend your weekly Strategic Planning time to 30-60 minutes. Revisit the Monthly Objectives every month and make any necessary changes to ensure you are going to reach your quarterly objectives.

QUARTERLY: Once per quarter, extend your weekly Strategic Planning time to 2-4 hours. Revisit your 12-month objectives and push them back out to 12 months. This is a 12-Month Revolving Strategic Plan, not one that sits on your shelf until next year.

ANNUALLY: Once a year, revisit your Vision, Mission, and Strategies, and make sure your whole plan is still pushing you toward your Business Maturity Date (Exit Strategy). Revisit your 12-month objectives and push them back out to 12 months.

If you want to learn more about this Strategic Plan, get a copy of *Making Money is Killing Your Business* by Chuck Blakeman.

Create a System for Marketing Your Products or Services

I took a marketing course a couple of years ago that taught a brilliant concept that stuck with me: The FEBE system. [2]

FEBE stands for Front End and Back End offers.

The Front End offer is how you attract porte clients into your email list: a download, a newsletter subscription, a free email course. The Back End offer is what you sell them after they are in your database. Remember that your most precious possession, your ring of power, is your database.

The Back End is where you make money because the toughest part is getting new clients. It's at least three times easier to sell to an existing customer than getting a new one.

You must create a repeatable process that brings clients in (front end) and keeps them in (back end). Each strategy is different. What you do to attract clients is different to what you do to keep them.

Why? Because at the front end you have to give a lot of value for free or almost free to gain peoples' trust. You don't try to sell anything at the front end, you just show them what you do to help them.

If you ask something, it's low risk. Perhaps just their email, or to follow you on social media.

Once you have built some trust and you are ready to make the first offer, it has to be so valuable, so darn ridiculous that you would give so much value for so little, that they won't be able to say no.

They would be crazy not to try it.

Aim to get as many clients as you can get up front so you can build trust and gather some testimonials from the get-go.

Go crazy, get different, do whatever you need to do to get them in. If you know your customer's lifetime value, how much he or she will spend with you through time, then you'll know how much you can invest to get one client.

The key is having a series of products that increase in cost so you can calculate how much you would make if someone buys them all.

Let's say the lifetime value of one client is $1,000. It would not make sense to spend $2,000 acquiring a customer then. But if the lifetime value is $10,000, then spending those $2,000 wouldn't be a problem.

In the frontend you can offer educational content. Most people these days give away ebooks or digital gifts (webinar or masterclass, a special report). Look at what other people are offering in your industry and create something different and better. What if you send them a physical book or a bottle of wine? If you know the lifetime value, you can know if it's worth it.

Do this now:

- Write down your crazy offer to get people to try your services.

- List the products or services you will offer as a funnel, with the cheapest on top, and the most expensive at the bottom. Add 3 to 6 products to the backend.
- Determine the Lifetime Value of a customer who goes through the whole funnel.

Keep it Simple

If you're just starting out, you don't have to have all the systems in place by tomorrow. Take your time and keep it simple.

As a solopreneur you will have to wear a lot of hats and do a bunch of stuff in your business. Just make sure you don't get consumed by the tyranny of the urgent and leave room for the priority of the important.

I like the advice from Megan Bowen to solopreneurs just starting out: build your reputation and build relationships.

Begin to cultivate a reputation, so that people know that you exist, what you stand for, what you offer and provide today. For instance, LinkedIn is a great platform to build your reputation.

"So step one," Megan says, "is really clarifying for yourself, who am I, what am I doing? What is my point of view? And then it's just getting started and not overthinking it at the beginning. People see Chris's videos on LinkedIn and they think, 'Oh, it's so slick and polished.' But when he first started doing this, he didn't get a lot of likes, he didn't get a lot of engagement. We all start somewhere and then it's being willing to dedicate the time and the commitment and the patience that's required to really build up some traction there."

The second step is building relationships. Think how

you can meet other people in your space, people that are talking to your customers but offering different services. Get to know those people so that they will recommend you or send you referrals.

"I think it really comes back to cultivating your own perspective and getting that out into the world and starting to build relationships with the right people who may be able to make connections for you."

Just as we learned to turn happy clients into referral sources, you can turn your connections into strategic partners.

Strategic partners are people who may never buy from you, but have all the clients you want and will send them your way as they begin to trust you.

The amazing thing is that you only need 5-15 strategic partners, along with your existing clients, to create a steady stream of potential clients.

If you want to identify a good strategic partner, ask yourself this question: What other business owner has the same customer base as me, but isn't competing with my company?

Describe your ideal strategic alliance partner. Make a list of several of them. Then ask yourself: What do they or their businesses need? How can I help them get there?

Serving them will set you apart from everyone else! Want an alliance? Serve them, and don't look for them to serve you first.

Checklist

☑ I have decided to play the business owner's game of making more money in less time.

☑ I have started to delegate, eliminate, and automate tasks to free my time.

☑ I have developed a 2-page strategic plan for growing my business.

☑ I have set up a FEBE system for marketing my products and services.

☑ I am building my reputation where my clients are.

☑ I am obtaining strategic partners by serving others in my network.

STEP 7
THE SOLO AUTHOR

Write a book or create an IP with your own system

Chapter 9

If you want to be president, you should write a book.

I'm not kidding. These are some U.S. presidents whose books helped them in their campaigns:

Dwight Eisenhower, Crusade in Europe (1948)

John F. Kennedy: Profiles in Courage (1956)

Richard Nixon: Six Crises (1962)

Barack Obama: Dreams from My Father (1995)

Donald Trump: Crippled America (2015)

Even Hitler wrote Mein Kampf in 1925 outlining his political ideology.

What is true for aspiring presidents, is true for thought leaders. Books are the new business cards. A published author can charge larger speaking and consulting fees than someone without a book in his or her name. In fact, event organizers, talk show hosts and podcasters prefer to invite authors to their shows over other guests.

Unfair? Maybe. But that's how it works. A book is a branding device that turns:

- a business executive into a thought leader
- a coach or consultant into an expert
- a solopreneur into sought-after advisor

And the book doesn't need to be a bestseller or a Pulitzer Prize winner. Because when you use your book to create your brand and market your services, your audience is not just the readers, but investors, speaking agents, and corporate clients.

Jaime Jay says his book, *Quit Repeating Yourself*, has helped him raise capital for his company. "Wow, putting a book out has opened a lot of doors," he says. "I know the same things now that when I wrote the book, but now all of a sudden I'm like a thought leader in the systems, processes, and the distant assistance arena. It's pretty amazing what a book will do."

Viveka agrees. And although she acknowledges it is very unlikely you will make a lot of money through book sales, writing a book is not about making money. In fact, 99% of authors don't sell more than 80 copies of their books.

"The book is like your business card on steroids," Viveka says. "It's what a Ph.D. used to be. It's something that differentiates you from everybody else out there. Who's an expert? Everybody out there. Who's a guru? Everybody else out there. But if you've taken the time to write the book, then it separates you. That's another way I differentiated myself."

To be fair, Viveka acknowledges that she didn't market her book as much she could have done, so sales were not great.

If you want to make money directly from book sales, you'll have to put on your innovator hat and go beyond the traditional channels or methods—like the Category Pirates who have popularized mini ebooks and have become Amazon bestsellers with a few of them.

Apart from direct sales, there are other ways to make money with your book, like these six:

1. Consulting: a book gives consultants more visibility and authority.

2. Coaching: stand out from all the coaches out there with a published book.

3. Speaking Gigs: authors are more likely to be invited as speakers.

4. Selling Products: use your book to promote your products.

5. Workshops and Courses: make your course an introduction to your paid training programs.

6. Agency Clients: land big clients for your agency with the prestige from a book.

David Meerman Scott says his books have landed him numerous speaking gigs. "Somebody who's booking speakers or booking someone to run a training program at a company is going to say, 'Okay, we've got to find somebody for our conference to speak about marketing.' And they find ten people and nine of them do not have books. One of them is a bestselling author with several books. That's who they are going to hire."

One of those speaking gigs was for Tony Robbins' *Business Mastery Events*. "Tony and his people read one of my books, which originally got me an introduction to Tony. So, I don't think I would have had an opportunity to work with Tony if I didn't have a popular book."

What a Book Can Do for You

Unlike writing a novel, which comes from the desire to tell a story inside of you or express yourself through literature, writing a nonfiction book serves a higher purpose than the book itself.

What do I mean by that? Unless you are a professional writer making a living out of your books, the purpose of writing a nonfiction book is to use it as a marketing tool for your business and thought leadership.

For example, Robert Kiyosaki, author of Rich Dad, Poor Dad, used several of his books to promote his board game Cashflow, or his seminars.

A book will help you be recognized as an expert.

Paul Estes wrote *Gig Mindset: Reclaim Your Time, Reinvent Your Career, and Ride the Next Wave of Disruption* while still holding a corporate job. [1]

"A book solidifies your work," he says. "It also tells everybody exactly what you believe in. Without it, you're just a talking head. If you're a thought leader, you have to have a book, you have to be creating stuff. Otherwise, go back to Corporate America, where you can just sit in a room and pontificate, get paid money for talking, sitting around and bash other people's ideas, but not really creating a point of view." [2]

There are certainly people who have been able to become thought leaders without books, but if you're appealing to a business audience, a book is a stamp of approval that you've been able to put your thoughts together in such a way that it's become a book.

A book will help you gain authority and credibility.

"I think that writing a book elevates you," Viveka says. "It's kind of the cream rising to the top. People will see you took the time to formulate your ideas and write a book. That separates you from everybody else out there, especially since everyone's calling themselves experts today."

The credibility Viveka gained from the book helped her advance her career and become a trainer for LinkedIn. When her editor at the publishing house went to work at the training site lynda.com, he took Viveka with him. *Lynda.com* was later acquired by LinkedIn and became what is now *LinkedIn Learning.*

A book will help you revolutionize your industry and have others apply and replicate your ideas.

Author and thought leadership consultant, Denise Brosseau, advises aspiring thought leaders to codify their lessons learned and create intellectual property to differentiate themselves as thought leaders and create momentum for their ideas.

"Every year millions of thought leaders with amazing ideas successfully create bold initiatives, programs, and products, and many gain a successful following for those ideas," she writes. "But to build momentum for new ways of thinking, to reframe an industry or pioneer sustained evolutionary or revolutionary change, you need to document what you know into a system, methodology, process, protocol, or set of guiding principles so others can easily understand, get on board, and help you replicate your ideas." [3]

Brosseau suggests five steps to create intellectual property out of your framework:

1. Create a visual representation that is easy to understand.
2. Clearly document how to use that framework.
3. Give it a great name.
4. Show proof that it works.
5. Protect and control its use.

How to Write a Book

"I've always wanted to write a book," is a common reply from people when I tell them I'm an author. In fact, 81% of Americans feel that they have a book in them and should write it. That's about 266 million people and very few will even attempt it. Of those who take the plunge and start writing a book, only 3% will actually finish it.

Why is it so? The three usual suspects (excuses) are:

- They can't decide on a good idea for the book.
- They don't have time to write.
- They don't know where to start.

Let's look at each of those in more detail.

1. How do I come up with my book idea?

We already said that the book is just a tool. So, if the book is the medium, what is the end? That is the right starting point to come up with a book idea. Ask yourself:

1. What do you want to accomplish in your business or career? What is your ultimate goal?
2. Who do you need to reach to accomplish your objective? Who is your target audience?
3. What do you need to teach them or show them to make that happen?

The answer to the third question is your book idea. But first you must answer the other two.

Let me give a personal example. Some years ago I was running my own life coaching business in South America. Here's how I answered the questions:

1. My goal was to move from in-person seminars to online on-demand courses. That meant I was going to compete with

many other life coaches out there and I needed to establish myself as an expert. You may already be an expert on something, but unless you have published a book on the topic, it's hard to prove it.

2. I wanted to reach young professionals in their mid-20s and early-30s who were struggling with finding their purpose in life.

3. I needed to teach them how to create a plan for their lives and the steps to reach their life goals.

So, the idea for my book, *El Arte de Cumplir tus Sueños (The Art of Making your Dreams Come True),* was born.

The goal was not to make the book a bestseller but to promote my online courses (which had a higher price point than the book). I actually gave the ebook away for free on many occasions to generate leads for my courses, which were advertised inside the book.

However, the book itself provides a lot of value, so people who can't afford the course can still get a lot from reading it.

I was already speaking and writing blogs about the topic, so writing the book was easy. In fact, in my book writing online course, I teach my students how to turn their blogs into books.

See what I'm doing there? I'm using this chapter to promote my course without telling you to buy it, while still providing value. You can either decide that the information in the chapter is enough or you may be curious about the course and go to my website to find out more.

That's what a book can do for you as well.

What if you don't have a business goal but still want to write a book?

Then, think about this:

- Is there something you know (a process, a series of lessons, philosophy) that can help others?
- Is there a story worth telling (your career success, your startup growth) and lessons to be learned from that story?
- Is there a trend that will disrupt your industry and you have some insights about it?

In Step 2, I talked about developing a unique angle for your message, coming up with innovative ideas and using languaging to differentiate yourself as a solo thought leader. When you sit down to write a book, your ideas will take form, a particular shape that you didn't know was there before. Why? Because the act of writing will force your brain to organize your ideas into a structure or process that makes sense logically. Trying to explain your leading thoughts makes them clearer.

This is what the Category Pirates call creating a new framework—that is, a new way of thinking. These are the steps they suggest: [4]

- Take anything you have figured out how to do successfully in your life or business and break it apart into steps. Be very specific on each step.
- Name and claim each step to make it memorable. Take for example each chapter title in this book.
- Name and claim the whole framework. For example, The Solo Thought Leader, or The 4-Hour Work Week.

2. How do I find time to write a book?

It's amazing how the busiest people on the planet find time to do what they really want, like watching a sports match. They may be postponing important things for weeks, but suddenly there is an opening when a friend comes with tickets to a game or a concert.

Things get moved around or canceled. Whatever they need to do to make it to the event. Why? Because it's something they want to do, it's something fun and different that stimulates their amygdala (the part of the brain that is the center for emotions, emotional behavior, and motivation).

But writing a book? It sounds like a lot of hard work and the amygdala pulls away from it, just like some people do with exercise.

Have you heard of the phrase, "I don't have time to go to the gym" or "I don't have time to workout"?

There's not a strong motivation, you need a big "why" to do it; if not, it's easier to blame a lack of time. That's why you need to change your mindset with these tricks.

Let the Book Idea Grab Hold of You

Find an idea you are passionate about, one that resonates with your values and that defines your mission in life. Then imagine communicating that idea in a book and making a huge impact on others. Let that idea percolate in your mind as you go to bed each night or as you are commuting or working out.

Keep nurturing the idea in your mind, even if you haven't written a word. After a few days or weeks, the idea will make your hands itch, telling you to write it down, until you can't do anything but write.

Focus on the Outcomes of Publishing Your Book
How will you feel when you finish your book? What will the business outcomes be?

Perhaps more clients, being recognized as a thought leader, speaking engagements, new consulting and coaching opportunities at higher prices. Your book may feel like a lot of work today but it will bring great rewards tomorrow.

Associate the Process with Something Pleasurable
Neuroscience tells us that the greater motivators for human behavior are avoiding pain and gaining pleasure. So, to change your mindset and create the writing habit, you must associate pleasure with the process of writing your book. Here are three ideas:

- Use your most comfortable chair only for writing during the time you need to finish your book.
- If you love coffee or tea, drink a cup while sitting down to write.
- Reward yourself with something pleasurable (a snack, your favorite playlist) every time you enter your writing space.

That way, your brain will associate the process of writing with something positive and will look forward to it.

Make Writing a Priority
I wrote my second novel between 5 a.m. and 7 a.m. every day for 3 months. At 7:15 a.m. my two boys would wake up and I had to get the oldest ready for school while my wife took care of our toddler. At 8 a.m., I had to start working at my job.

I had a busy schedule as a parent, husband, employee, and more. But I made finishing my book a priority. That meant finding time to write when I had no interruptions or distractions.

It was 2009, and I was already working from home, so my best time to write was early in the morning, because:

Everyone at home was sleeping. My mind was fresh as I had no mental baggage from the day. No emails or messages from work would interrupt me at that time. It was a set time for the purpose of writing, so there was no need to multitask.

Waking up before sunrise was not always fun, but it was a commitment I made for those three months. I had a word count quota to meet every day and nothing was going to stop me from achieving that.

I think you have not written your book because of lack of time, but because it's not your priority... yet.

Finding the Best Time to Write

Are you a morning or a night person? When can you write with less distractions? Those are things you will have to consider when scheduling writing time in your calendar. But before setting the appointment with your book, you must find the best time to write.

Writing productivity coaches Bec Evans and Chris Smith came up with the traffic light scheduling technique, which is very useful to find out the times you can't write as well as those you can. [5] This is how it works:

- **Red Times:** Go through your diary and work out which periods of time in your week are totally out of bounds for writing. These are your red times, and they could be times when you're at work or busy with other stuff. Don't write during this time.

- **Yellow Times:** Look for the times in your week which are possible writing times. These are your yellow times. You might have a few distractions during these time slots, or you might be a little tired, but there's probably something you can do in those times, like research, or editing existing material.
- **Green Times:** These are times in your week which are clear for writing and that you can always commit to. Tell family and coworkers that green times are writing times and need to be respected. No interruptions allowed!

Add those times to your calendar in 45 to 90 minutes per day, with a break for sessions longer than 45 minutes.

At the end of the day, if you really want to write a book, you will find the time. Busier people than you are writing books and more. So, you can do it as well.

Perhaps the problem is deeper than that. Be honest with yourself: when in the foreseeable future will you have enough time to write a book?

Have you ever considered how much time it really takes to write and what would be the daily commitment? If you haven't, then you are just guessing and your guess is probably an overestimation.

What if I tell you that you only need to invest one hour per day (weekends off) during three months to finish your book? Is that too much to ask or can you commit to that?

3. Where do I start?

I wrote and self-published my book, E*l Arte de Cumplir tus Sueños*, in two weeks. It wasn't a short ebook, but a 168-page book, fully designed and published on Amazon as paperback and kindle. How did I do it?

- Narrowed down my idea (what is it about and who is it for?)
- Created an outline (chapter topics and all)
- Created a Notebook in Evernote and a separate note for each chapter
- Wrote the introduction (found a great story to start it off and set the tone of the book)
- Searched my files for articles, audios, speaking notes, and anything I could find that I had on the topic of each chapter and pasted that under each chapter note
- Organized and rewrote the existing materials to make it flow
- Filled in the gaps with new info, writing the first draft as fast as I could
- Walked away for a couple of days, and then went back to edit and polish
- Handed it over to my editor (my wife)
- Did the cover design, the layout, wrote the back cover copy
- Set everything up in Amazon's KDP and hit Publish

The above is just an eagle-eye's view of the process (without talking about the marketing). I could do it fast because I'm a professional writer and have worked in publishing before.

But I think that with the right guidance and blueprint, you can also do it. What you need is:

- A process to flesh out your book idea
- A process to structure your content
- A process to write regularly and meet your goals
- A process to write fast, edit thoroughly and publish right

Now, many aspiring authors ask: should I write it myself or hire a ghostwriter? It's a valid question.

Here are some PROS of hiring a ghostwriter:

- You don't have to commit time and energy to writing
- You don't have to learn the process of writing a book
- You make sure the book will be finished on time
- A professional writer will make you look good (hopefully)

And the CONS of hiring a ghostwriter:

- Good ghostwriters are expensive ($15k to $100k+)
- Great business ghostwriters are not easy to find and manage
- You take a big risk (you may not like the book and there is no money back guarantee)
- You are not the real author of your own book

If you can afford a ghostwriter with a good track record and don't mind taking credit for the work of someone else (even if they are your ideas), it is a viable option. But my advice is that you write it yourself.

After writing two novels and nine nonfiction books, I've learned a few proven lessons that can help you write a great book fast. I've developed a 7-step system to write your first business book in 90 days, even if you have little or no time to write, you're not a skilled writer, and your book idea is half-baked.

These are the 7 steps:

1. Start from the back.

- Refine your book idea—what to write about.
- Define who your target reader is.
- Create your value proposition.
- List the main benefits of the book.
- Develop a unique angle for your book.
- Learn how to write the back cover (or front flap) copy.

2. Outline your book.

- Create the Table of Contents.
- Define the structure of the book.
- Select chapter topics.
- Write chapter summaries.

3. Gather your sources.

- Turn your blog into a book if you have one.
- Incorporate and organize existing content into your draft (audio, video, etc.).
- Evaluate online sources and do research for your book.
- Interview experts and gather stories.

4. Structure your chapters.

- Outline each chapter with the CPE Method (see Step 4).
- Write hooks to capture the attention of your readers.

5. Prepare to write.

- Set up daily writing schedules and install writing tools.
- Prepare your writing cave and eliminate distractions.
- Organize your research files.

6. Apply the Button Method.

- Write the first draft fast, without editing.
- Deal effectively with writer's block.

7. Review your manuscript.

- Self-edit your draft.
- Prepare your manuscript for an editor.
- Research publishing options.

Check out all the info about the on-demand course and personalized book coaching at *diegopineda.ca*.

Checklist

☑   I have decided to write a book and create valuable intellectual property out of my ideas.

☑   I have landed a book idea that is aligned with my business goals.

☑   I have made writing my book a priority and have started working on it.

DREAMING IS GOOD. EXECUTING IS BETTER.

Chapter 10

What can you learn from the inventors of the hot air balloon? The secret to succeed as a solopreneur.

Joseph was the dreamer, the visionary. But he wasn't good at business or professional networking.

His brother, Jacques was the businessman, the executioner, with the skills that his older brother lacked. They were the perfect team.

The Montgolfier brothers dreamed of flying like the birds.

One day, Joseph observed how some clothes being dried by the fire began lifting toward the ceiling. Intrigued by this, he began experimenting with lifting light boxes with hot air.

Later, he convinced his brother to help him make a silk bag of 635 cubic feet. In December, 1782 they tested their bag and it reached an altitude of 820 feet.

The following summer they made the first public demonstration. They burned wood and hay beneath the opening of a balloon that reached an altitude of 6,500 feet and landed 1.2 miles away after 10 minutes in the air.

The news spread around France and they were invited to Paris to perform more tests. Jacques, with his entrepreneurial spirit, found an expert paper maker to help them build a balloon of more than 3,500 cubic feet.

On September, 19, 1783, before King Louis XVI and the queen, they launched the first balloon carrying passengers: a sheep, a duck and a rooster. The balloon flew for 8 minutes and landed safely 2 miles away.

A month later they launched an even bigger balloon (60,000 cubic feet), with passengers on board, but tied to the ground. After this success, they decided to make the first manned balloon flight in November that year.

Louis XVI wanted the passengers to be condemned criminals but a scientist and an army officer requested the honor of being the pilots. They traveled 5 miles over Paris and landed outside the city after 25 minutes of flight.

You know, this amazing story illustrates the elements that you need to create a plan for your life and fulfill your dreams.

It's not enough to dream dreams. Joseph the dreamer needed Jacques the businessman. Thanks to Jacques, the hot air balloon went from a private hobby to an invention that revolutionized the world.

The Montgolfier brothers progressively scaled their achievements, formed a team with other people, conducted marketing and PR to attract the attention of the French royalty, and experimented with various sizes and animals, before attempting human flight.

If they hadn't followed those steps, perhaps they would have never invented the hot air balloon nor received an award from the French Academy of Sciences.

What is the lesson?

That execution must overshadow even the grandest vision.

Dream big. Execute 10x bigger.

You need ideas, lots of them. Ideas for how to improve your business, solve your clients' problems, transform your industry, leave a legacy. Ideas to find your creative voice and style, ideas to communicate your message and educate your audience.

Those ideas, however, need to be accompanied by massive action. That's where your strategic plan will come in handy to show you what you have to do every day to reach your goals. Let it be your Yoda. It will guide you well.

Dealing with Fears and Imposter Syndrome

Solopreneurs must face different fears along the way to thought leadership: fear of failure, fear of rejection, fear of being vulnerable, fear of letting others down, and even fear of success.

Perhaps you fear that you won't be seen as an expert, because there are others that know more than you or have been in the field for longer.

Perhaps you doubt that your point of view is unique enough and others have already said what you have to say.

Or perhaps you hold yourself back because of your age, or your perceived lack of education or job titles in your resume.

Or the most common fear of all: imposter syndrome, which affects even those at the top.

Research shows that 70% of high achieving women suffer from this phenomenon, which makes them believe they don't deserve their accomplishments and that they are intellectual frauds. They fear being recognized as impostors and suffer from anxiety, fear of failure and dissatisfaction with life. [1]

But it's not only women. Men also report feeling this way.

It may affect you if during your journey to become a solo expert you realize how much you don't know and you compare yourself to others who started before you. It may affect you if your solopreneur habits of doing everything by yourself hit a wall and you feel that asking for help makes you a failure.

And it may destroy you if you are a perfectionist who is never satisfied, no matter how much you accomplish in your business or career.

Justin Welsh says he feels like that every single day, but he reframes it in a positive manner.

"If you have an imposter syndrome, there are generally two things happening," he says. "The first thing that's happening is you're doing well at something because you can't have impostor syndrome if you're a failure, right? You have to be having some sort of success to start feeling imposter syndrome. So that's a good thing."

Most people who have imposter syndrome are successful, so you are in good company.

"The other thing is that I have friends who are rich and successful and they're all just really regular guys and girls. They don't have an extremely deep skill set. They just work hard. They try things, they experiment. They're humble, they're consistent, they go for it. And I have conversations with them and I realize everyone's just figuring it out, trying to get through each day and figure out something new. What you see online is just a sliver of their life, their success, how they work. So, just recognize that behind the curtain every successful person doubts themselves."

Never Stop Growing and Innovating

In *Play Bigger: How Pirates, Dreamers, and Innovators Create and Dominate Markets*, the authors make the case for never settling down, but once you establish yourself as the expert or the best in your field, to keep expanding your category.

"Amazon started by selling books, nailed that, and then expanded to other areas of retail. It didn't start on day one saying it would be the next generation's most powerful retailer. Legendary category kings constantly look for ways to expand their categories, increasing their category potential. It's good advice for people, too. This is how you grow, open up new opportunities, and generate more demand for yourself. If you become the category king of product designers in a small company, maybe it's time to move to a bigger company. If you're the best kitchen remodeler in town, maybe it's time to tackle whole-house remodeling. Build on your position and move outward and upward, looking for a need that fits your skills or acquiring the skills to fit a need." [2]

It's not going to be easy though. Critics will call you crazy and those who love the status quo will dismiss you. But keep going.

Becoming a solo thought leader means forging your own path. It's not even the road less traveled. It's exploring new frontiers, or like Captain Kirk would say, "going where no man has gone before." [3]

Let me end with a quick story.

My first book was rejected multiple times by traditional publishers. Why? Because it didn't fit a rigid category.

Do Vaccines Cause That?! (2008), which I co-authored with an M.D. was about the science of vaccine safety for concerned parents. Academic publishers said it was too light for them; generic publishers said it was too technical.

They would not take the risk despite our solid marketing plan, a website with 50,000 visitors per month, and partners willing to buy copies across the United States. So, we self-published and sold the first print run of 5,000 copies within a year.

Something similar happened with my first novel. My literary agent could not sell it because publishers thought it was too controversial (the plot showed how political agendas can influence scientific theories). And about the second novel they said: "Beautifully written, but it might offend some readers."

Publishers want to know where to safely place you among the sections of a bookstore. But there's a reason I have self-published 90% of my books, including this one: I love to come up with ideas that can't sit neatly on a shelf, but jump out and slap people in the face.

I refuse to be boxed in. And perhaps you are also like that: different, rebel, crazy. Weird.

That's why I like you. The world needs more weird people. Now go and freak everybody out with your awesomeness.

The Solo Thought Leader's Manifesto

Remember that quote in Step 5 about not calling yourself a thought leader? I think it's partially true.

Yes, you should not be changing your LinkedIn headline to "Thought Leader" or make it your official title (although Chief Thought Leader doesn't sound bad, right?).

However, just between you and I, you should believe it and call yourself a solo thought leader—at least in private. Our self-talk, what we say to ourselves in our inner conversations, is powerful and manifests in the physical. So, go ahead and think of yourself as a solo thought leader.

If your goal is really to become an expert in your niche and make a lasting impact in the world as a business of one, then here's the Solo Thought Leader's Manifesto for you:

I am a Solo Thought Leader.
I am the go-to expert in my field.
I innovate and design categories.
I educate to transform people's lives.
And make the world a better place.
I don't compete with others,
I am the only one.

What's next?

The journey from solopreneur to thought leader is exciting and rewarding, but it requires hard work and patience. The good news is that you don't have to go it alone.

Now that you've read this book, you have a better view of the steps you need to take. There are a lot of things you may need to work on and figure out.

I suggest you go through the checklists at the end of each chapter and mark them as complete as you accomplish each milestone. You can also take an online version of the checklist at *solothoughtleader.com/score*

I've included other valuable free resources in that page as well that will help you achieve your goals faster.

If you have any questions or feedback about this book, please email me at: diego@solothoughtleader.com.

I will personally respond to your email.

Follow me on Twitter: @DiegoPinedaVL

Let's connect on LinkedIn: linkedin.com/in/dipineda

Notes

Chapter 1

1. Godin, Seth. Permission Marketing: Turning Strangers into Friends and Friends into Customers. Simon & Schuster, New York, 1999.

2. Godin, 1999.

3. See sethgodin.com

4. The New York Public Library (2022, January 23). Clark Terry, NYPL jazz oral history [Video]. YouTube. https://youtu.be/Gs7scf4nymU

5. Collins, Jim. Good to Great. Harper Collins, New York, 2001.

6. Shriner-Cahn, David. (2021, December 15). Personal communication [Personal interview].

7. Kotler, Steven. The Art of Impossible: A Peak Performance Primer. Harper Collins, New York, 2021.

8. Kotler, 2021.

9. Scott, David M. (2021, November 8). Personal communication [Personal interview].

Chapter 2

1. Altucher, James. Think Like a Billionaire. Scribd Editions, 2019.

2. Patel, Neil. "How to Dominate Google in 2021". Neil Patel's Blog. November 2021. https://neilpatel.com/blog/google-ranking/

3. "Nick". (2021, November 3). Personal communication [Personal interview].

4. Bowen, Megan. (2021, December 15). Personal communication [Personal interview].

5. Blakeman, Chuck. *Making Money is Killing Your Business*. Crankset Group, 2010.

Chapter 3

1. von Rosen, Viveka. (2021, November 4). Personal communication [Personal interview].

2. Chan, Marcus. (2021, December 9). Personal communication [Personal interview].

3. Economy, Peter. "Tony Robbins: 19 Inspiring Power Quotes for Success". Inc. January 2022. https://www.inc.com/peter-economy/tony-robbins-19-inspiring-power-quotes-for-success.html

4. Friedman, Ron. *Decoding Greatness: How the Best in the World Reverse Engineer Success.*. Simon & Schuster, 2021.

5. Welsh, Justin. (2021, November 8). Personal communication [Personal interview].

6. Maxwell, John. "The Three Types of Mentors Every Person Needs to Help Them Grow." John Maxwell's Blog. April 5, 2016. https://www.johnmaxwell.com/blog/the-three-types-of-mentors-every-person-needs-to-help-them-grow/

7. Epstein, David. *Range: How Generalists Triumph in a Specialized World*. Pan MacMillan, 2019.

8. Epstein, 2019.

Chapter 4

1. Scott, David M. (2021, November 8). Personal communication [Personal interview].

2. Diamandis, Peter. "Use Google's 8 Innovation Principles in Your Startup". October 14, 2021. https://www.diamandis.com/blog/use-googles-principles-in-your-startup

3. Mattimore, Brian. *21 Days to a Big Idea!* Diversion Books, 2015.

4. Wilkinson, Amy. The Creator's Code: The Six Essential Skills of Extraordinary Entrepreneurs. Simon & Schuster, New York, 2015.

5. Goodwin, Bob. (2021, November 29). Personal communication [Personal interview].

6. Arms, John. (2021, December 13). Personal communication [Personal interview].

7. Lakhiani, Vishen. The Code of the Extraordinary Mind. Simon & Schuster, New York, 2016.

Chapter 5

1. NBC New York Channel 4. "Tony Robbins Loves Profanity," https://www.nbcnewyork.com/news/national-international/tony-robbins-2/2162979/

2. Griffin, Michelle. (2021, November 28). Personal communication [Slack Message].

3. Languaging: The Strategic Use of Language to Change Thinking. Category Pirates Newsletter. https://categorypirates.substack.com/p/languaging-the-strategic-use-of-language

4. Jay, Jaime. (2021, November 23). Personal communication [Personal interview].

Chapter 6

1. Robinson, Ken. The Element: How Finding Your Passion Changes Everything. Penguin, London, 2009.

2. Scott, David M. (2021, November 8). Personal communication [Personal interview].

3. Burnes, Rick. "Study Shows Business Blogging Leads to 55% More Website Visitors." HubSpot Blog. https://blog.hubspot.com/blog/tabid/6307/bid/5014/study-shows-business-blogging-leads-to-55-more-website-visitors.aspx

4. LeFever, Lee. The Art of Explanation. Wiley, New York, 2012.

5. Adgate, Brad. "As Podcasts Continue to Grow In Popularity, Ad Dollars Follow."Forbes. https://www.forbes.com/sites/bradadgate/2021/02/11/podcasting-has-become-a-big-business/?sh=6d5635002cfb

6. Borges, Bernie. (2021, December 17). Personal communication [Personal interview].

7. Shriner-Cahn, David. (2021, December 15). Personal communication [Personal interview].

8. Olafson, Karen and Tran, Tony. 100+ Social Media Demographics that Matter to Marketers in 2021. Hootsuite. January 27, 2021. https://blog.hootsuite.com/social-media-demographics/

9. Reich, Justin and Ruipérez-Valiente, José A. "The MOOC pivot." January 2019 Science, 363(6423):130-131. DOI:10.1126/science.aav7958

Chapter 7

1. Vajre, Sangram. "3 Reasons You Should Never Call Yourself a Thought Leader." Inc. May 22, 2017. https://www.inc.com/sangram-vajre/3-reasons-you-should-never-call-yourself-a-thought-leader.html

2. Hennessy, Brittany. Influencer: Building Your Personal Brand in the Age of Social Media. Citadel, 2018.

Chapter 8

1. Blakeman, Chuck. Making Money is Killing Your Business. Crankset Group, 2010.

2. Eker, T Harv. The Wealthy Marketer [Online Course]. https://www.harvekeronline.com/twm/letter/100off/

Chapter 9

1. Estes, Paul. Gig Mindset: Reclaim Your Time, Reinvent Your Career, and Ride the Next Wave of Disruption. Lioncrest Publishing, 2019.
2. Estes, Paul. (2022, January 3). Personal communication [Personal interview].
3. Brosseau, Denise. Ready to Be a Thought Leader?: How to Increase Your Influence, Impact, and Success. Wiley, 2013.
4. Category Pirates. "How To Write A Top 1% Business Newsletter: 7 Ways To Differentiate Your Content." https://categorypirates.substack.com/p/how-to-write-a-top-1-business-newsletter
5. Evans, Bec. "Finding time to write: the time boxer." Prolifiko. https://prolifiko.com/time-boxer/

Chapter 10

1. Sakulku, J. (1). The Impostor Phenomenon. The Journal of behavioural science, 6 (1), 75-97. https://doi.org/10.14456/ijbs.2011.6
2. Ramadan, Al. Play Bigger: How Pirates, Dreamers, and Innovators Create and Dominate Markets. HarperCollins, 2016.
3. Star Trek Television Series. Paramount Television, 1969.

About the Author

Diego Pineda is the author of two novels, 9 non-fiction books, and hundreds of articles and blogs as a science writer, a business writer, and a sales and marketing writer.

He started his career as a medical writer while writing fiction on the side.

He is also a book coach helping solopreneurs and business leaders write their first book fast so they can become thought leaders in their industries, gain authority and visibility, and make more money.

He and his wife, Diana, live in British Columbia, Canada, with their son, Daniel.